THE POWER OF THE STORY

THE VOICE OF WITNESS TEACHER'S GUIDE TO ORAL HISTORY

COMPILED AND EDITED BY
CLIFF MAYOTTE

WITH A FOREWORD BY
RICHARD AYERS
AND WILLIAM AYERS

VOICE OF WITNESS

VOICE OF WITNESS

M^cSWEENEY'S BOOKS
SAN FRANCISCO

For more information about McSweeney's, see www.mcsweeneys.net
For more information about Voice of Witness, see www.voiceofwitness.org

Second Edition. Copyright © 2013 McSweeney's and Voice of Witness

CONTENTS

Voice of Witness is excited to offer the second edition of this resource to educators. The goals of this two-part guide are to provide educators with the tools and resources for teaching oral histories from the Voice of Witness book series in the classroom, and to provide step-by-step instructions for the creation of oral history projects with students. The "target audience" for the guide **is primarily grades 9–12,** with many lesson plans that are suitable for middle-school students. Our goal in creating this guide is to facilitate meaningful teaching and learning through the compelling lens of oral history. Since VOW's inception in 2004, teachers in the United States and around the world have used the evocative narratives from our book series to explore contemporary issues in the classroom.

We have shown that there are stories everywhere, and people in every corner of the world who long to be heard. Through Voice of Witness, students have met individuals like Ma Su Mon, a courageous young Burmese journalist; Patricia Thompson, a survivor of Hurricane Katrina; and Abel, a Guatemalan who encountered systematic workplace abuse at the hands of his employers. Their stories adeptly illustrate oral history's ability to put a human face on issues and events, giving students a nuanced, reality-based understanding not found in most mainstream narratives. And that is ultimately what Voice of Witness does: it allows those who are ignored, marginalized, and stripped of their humanity to finally tell their stories. To bear witness, to be counted and named, to have their identity reclaimed through storytelling. But there is something else at work when one encounters these oral histories—a capacity to be transformed by the power of the story.

Through our education program, we have seen firsthand how these stories have achieved instant "buy in" with students, inspiring compassion, outrage, and a deep connection to what it is to be human. Our oral history training for students has likewise shown us that oral history projects empower students with an inclusive and participatory vision of the world.

The same goes for educators—using narratives from the series and guiding students through the oral history process can be a liberating experience. This process encourages genuine collaboration, allowing teachers to create lessons and projects *with* students, rather than just *for* them. An oral history classroom that fosters listening without judgment and with compassion creates an environment that is open-ended, question-based, and intensely democratic. These are the critical thinking skills and habits of mind that teachers have valued in the Voice of Witness series and the reason we have been inspired to create this resource. This second edition includes a new section on exile and displacement, additional lesson plans, and expanded, updated resources.

We like to think of the lessons and activities in this book as blueprints with various points of entry, as opposed to a prescriptive guide that needs to be followed to the letter. Imagine the resource as a dialogue between educators, with plenty of space created for new ideas and approaches. All of this to say that no curriculum is ever truly definitive, so we encourage educators to adapt the lesson plans in the book to suit the needs of their students. Voice of Witness welcomes suggestions and feedback as part of our commitment to providing useful and relevant oral history–based curriculum to U.S. schools. Together, we can harness the power of the story as a vital tool in creating a more empathic society, giving students an opportunity to understand the world more completely.

Dave Eggers
Cofounder
Voice of Witness

Cliff Mayotte
Education Program Director
Voice of Witness

ABOUT VOICE OF WITNESS

Voice of Witness is a non-profit organization that uses oral history to illuminate contemporary human rights crises in the U.S. and around the world. Founded by author Dave Eggers and physician/human rights scholar Lola Vollen, Voice of Witness publishes a book series that depicts human rights injustices through the stories of the men and women who experience them. The Voice of Witness Education Program brings these stories, and the issues they reflect, into high schools and impacted communities through oral history-based curricula and holistic educator support.

ACKNOWLEDGMENTS

PRIMARY WRITER: Cliff Mayotte
ASSISTANT EDITORS: John Knight, Claire Kiefer

Voice of Witness would like to acknowledge the following educators for their contributions to this guide. Their commitment to teaching and learning is present on every page.

Cheryl Nelson, *John O'Connell High School, San Francisco, CA*

Eileen O'Kane, *Immaculate Conception Academy, San Francisco, CA*

Lisa Morehouse

Michael Rosenberg, *Balboa High School*

Trevor Gardner, *Envision Academy, Oakland, CA*

Katherine Geers, *Mission San Jose High School, Fremont, CA*

Jennifer Moore, *Mission San Jose High School*

Anne Grajeda, *Envision Academy*

Joe Chellino, *Joliet West High School, Joliet, IL*

Denise Savoy, *San Francisco Community School*

Stephanie Sotomayor, *Oceana High School, Pacifica, CA*

Michael Sudmeier

Stacey Goodman, *The Athenian School, Danville, CA*

Mark Heringer, *Academy of Arts and Sciences, San Francisco School of the Arts*

Mark Davis, *Facing History and Ourselves*

Charlotte Crowe

Kathryn Kuszmar, *Notre Dame High School, San Jose, CA*

Bill Pratt, *Berkeley High School, Berkeley, CA*

Lauren Markham, *Oakland International High School, Oakland, CA*

Robert Sanborn, *Lick-Wilmerding High School, San Francisco, CA*

VOICE OF WITNESS EDUCATION PROGRAM ADVISORY:
Richard Ayers, *University of San Francisco School of Education*

William Ayers *University of Illinois at Chicago (emeritus)*

Nishat Kurwa, *Youth Radio*

Gerald Richards, *CEO 826 National*

Kathryn Kuszmar, *Notre Dame High School, San Jose, CA*

VOICE OF WITNESS:
FOUNDING EDITORS: Dave Eggers and Lola Vollen

EXECUTIVE DIRECTOR/EXECUTIVE EDITOR: mimi lok

MANAGING EDITOR: Luke Gerwe

DEVELOPMENT AND COMMUNICATIONS DIRECTOR: Juliana Sloane

EDUCATION PROGRAM DIRECTOR: Cliff Mayotte

PUBLICITY ASSOCIATE: McKenna Stayner

EDUCATION ASSOCIATE: Claire Kiefer

This project was made possible with the generous support of the Hemera Foundation.

EVERY PERSON IS A PHILOSOPHER/
EVERY DAY IS ANOTHER STORY

by William Ayers and Richard Ayers

This teaching guide initiates a collegial discussion among teachers and within communities. It is an invitation to take off from some excellent teaching projects that have already been piloted, and then to go further, to invent your own way in.

Oral history can be a truly revolutionary pedagogy. Because the work is propelled by questions instead of answers, it liberates students from the dull routines of passively receiving predigested information. Instead, they become actors in constructing history and contributing substantively to the trajectory of the curriculum. They invent and experience the method of science, proposing explanations of the world, and then investigate to test the truth or to modify their explanations.

Students can approach the work as artists, filled with creativity and inventiveness, generative mistakes and sparkling epiphanies. Teachers can learn to take an attentive and supportive backseat, after sufficient preparation, and watch democratic education emerge from projects that the students themselves have learned to own. Through these projects, the stories that have been hidden, suppressed, and ignored begin to take center stage, and the real dimensions of one's community and its struggles burst forth and grab the mic. This is why oral history, in form and content, can become a central project of social justice in our classrooms.

Oral history concerns itself with what happened, and with an essential overlap: that which is *said* to have happened. Oral historians do the work, then, of historians—sifting through the records for facts and artifacts—as well as the work of anthropologists—searching for the meanings that people attribute to particular events and specific experiences. By doing both, and then some, oral historians gather together the factual and the meaningful.

The focus of oral history, like the focus of great teaching, is always the *space between*: between history and anthropology, happening and narrative, fact and meaning, past and present, remembering and forgetting, student and teacher, interviewer and subject. Oral history is not an adjunct or a poor cousin to "real" history. Nor is it pure fiction, an imaginary tale spun out with no relationship to any external referent whatsoever. Rather, it is a necessary third *thing* with its own integrity, demands, traditions, and base: it is engaged in a history of moments, as well as interested in a history of memory.

For the oral historian, like the teacher, the task is to question, question, question—and after that, to question some more. The approach to teaching oral history found in this book and in the Voice of Witness series offers a break with the tendency in American culture toward narcissism and passivity.

It is outward looking. It seeks answers in the wisdom of others. It also inspires us to examine what makes people tick, what makes our complex world so exciting and confusing, who we are, where we have come from, and where we are headed.

The oral history interview is always a dialogue: someone is telling a story to someone else. Like any other dialogue, and like teaching at its best, it depends on relationship more than technique.

The interview is not an interrogation or an intrusion, or a designated therapeutic moment; it is rather the opening of a narrative space that people may choose to enter or not. It is an invitation, not a destination. The interviewer, like the engaged teacher, is the student, the learner, the one who brings a lack of knowledge and a certain ignorance into the conversation; the subject of the interview, or the narrator, is the teacher, the recognized authority, and an entire universe of meaning-making energy. For the interviewer, listening actively and attentively is the main idea; learning from the stories of a range of participants is the payoff. For the narrator, the conversation is another occasion to perform an account of events and experiences for an audience, a chance to reveal meanings, and in the process discover something valuable and possibly new.

When we think of oral narratives as performances, we allow a different order of response. Someone in the United States says, "I don't remember those bad times," and we note that forgetting can be psychologically understandable, even when politically unstable. Someone begins a commentary by noting, "I'm a black man," or "I'm a woman," or "I'm transgendered," or "As a refugee." In some settings this may invite critique or correction, but for oral historians it provokes a primary question: *Why begin from that standpoint? What is the meaning of this positioning to what is to follow? What can we learn that we do not know from the decision to utter that very sentence?*

Oral history is the poetry of the everyday, the literature of the streets, the subjective experiences and personal perspectives of the extraordinary ordinary people—not a substitute but an essential piece of any accurate record of human events. The creators of the Voice of Witness series, and the approaches offered in this guide, allow students as oral historians to reject the dispassionate stance of traditional social science, adopting instead a capacity for empathy and identification, for greater joy and immense indignation and, above all, a willingness to be changed in the process.

The stories people tell and share can become powerful tools against propaganda, political dogmas, and all manner of impositions and stereotypes. Seeking honesty and authenticity in stories means becoming attuned, as well, to contradiction, disagreements, silences, negation, denials, inconsistencies, confusion, challenges, turmoil, puzzlement, commotion, ambiguities, paradoxes, disputes, uncertainty, and every kind of muddle. Oral historians, like teachers, dive headfirst into the wide, wild world of human experience.

TRANSFORMATION THROUGH THE STORIES OF OTHERS

by Lola Vollen, cofounder, Voice of Witness

———————

Fatima's story changed my life. I met her by chance in 1996, a year after the end of the war in Bosnia—a war in which her son went missing. My life has never been the same since she told me what happened to her family in the final days of the war. The Voice of Witness book series harnesses the transformative power of such first hand accounts in order to powerfully illuminate the human rights and social justice issues of our time.

Our education program is not only a teacher resource for using such accounts in meaningful ways, but also a comprehensive guide for teachers who want to enable their students to elicit and document meaningful narratives through a thoughtful interviewing process and create powerful oral history projects of their own.

Fatima's son had been a victim of the 1995 ethnic cleansing of Srebrenica—ironically the first U.N. declared "safe haven"—in which nearly 8,000 Muslim men and boys had been summarily executed by Serb forces. The response of the international community was to establish a war crimes tribunal, which began unearthing the mass graves of Srebrenica's victims for the sole purpose of collecting evidence for the prosecution of those responsible for Europe's worst atrocity since the holocaust.

At that time, I was in Bosnia on a routine medical mission to rebuild its public health system. I had read about the fall of Srebrenica, even visited the eerily deserted city and wandered its empty streets still strewn with the remnants of the pillaging of its homes and storefronts. But the plight of the missing and their survivors was not part of my Bosnian landscape.

Fatima still hoped to find her son alive. But if he was dead, she told me, all she wanted was his bones so she could do in death what she could not do in his lifetime—care and protect all that remained of him. What I learned from my encounter with Fatima and other women with missing family was what these survivors needed to move on with their lives—they needed to know with certainty the fate of their missing members and have their individually-identified remains returned to them for proper burial.

Before Fatima, I had never spoken to a survivor from Srebrenica, much less wondered what they needed to get on with their lives. After meeting Fatima, I assumed that in the aftermath of such an unconscionable atrocity there would be an all-out endeavor to address the needs of its survivors. But there wasn't. No one was asking or listening to what the survivors had to say.

Because I did, I ended up staying in Bosnia from 1996 to 2000 with Physicians for Human Rights, to work with the survivors from Srebrenica, developing and directing the largest-ever mass grave exhumation and identification program for families whose loved ones went missing in the war. What I heard from listening to Fatima and other survivors of Srebrenica made me stay and do what I did.

I am not the first person to have their life transformed by personal accounts of injustice. Nor was Fatima's the first or last personal account to take me to places in my own life I had never imagined going. During my first summer off from college, it was Studs Terkel who brought first hand narratives to my doorstep. I remember well the impact of one bundle of his stories that arrived in the mail under the title *Working*.

House sitting, working as a waitress, busboy, and computer board assembler—the first-person accounts in *Working* revealed the intricacies and richness of life in blue collar America. This was hardly the vista I enjoyed from my perch just outside of Harvard Square, but, captivated by the lives and life forces revealed in *Working*, the experience of reading the book was pivotal for me: everyone Studs introduced me to—farmers, waitresses, taxi drivers, truck drivers—were interesting people to me, and a new sense that the richness of life was omnipresent to those who knew how to tap it began to take root. And *Working* gave me the framework to perceive the richness, meaning, and pleasure of my own summertime gigs.

It was at a Studs Terkel event in 2003 that I met Dave Eggers. By that time, my life had been snagged by yet another story—that of Herman Atkins, a man wrongfully convicted of rape who spent twelve years in prison before he was finally exonerated. He was released with nothing but the clothes on his back to join a growing and marginalized population of the formerly incarcerated. By 2003, I had collected interviews of over 50 exonerated victims of our criminal justice system, many of whom had been on death row. Once again, I was astounded to find that what I came to view as a great injustice was largely being ignored.

Herman's story, like Fatima's story, made me want to do something and, as in Bosnia, what I did was start a program—the Life After Exoneration Program—to address the needs of this growing, but invisible, population of exonerees. As a public health physician, program development was part of my repertoire—this is what public health people do. But I was frustrated at my inability to harness on their behalf the very force that compelled my dedication to their needs—the power of their stories. I carried their stories in my head, wishing others could share the burden of knowing, until I met a man with the bullhorn ready to broadcast them. Dave was eager and able to publish these stories and together we launched the Voice of Witness book series, harnessing the transformational power of first person accounts to convey the profoundly unsettling realities of life for today's victims of systemic injustice and abuse.

Educational programming began in 2007, working initially with a handful of local teachers. These teachers quickly discovered that they could engage their students in new and exciting ways by incorporating the narratives from the Voice of Witness series into their curriculum. We took a giant step forward when we partnered with Facing History and Ourselves, an international organization known for innovative professional development and humanities education, to develop classroom-based oral history projects In 2009, Cliff Mayotte brought his nearly 25 years of experience to bear on these pilot projects that involved over 750 students. Cliff provided students and faculty the framework, skills, and support necessary to responsibly tap into and document the rich reservoir of human experience to be discovered through thoughtful interviewing and curated by skilled editing.

As a physician caring for patients, I consider myself lucky to have ongoing access to personal narratives. Since medical school I have focused on the "art" and practice of the clinical interview. Stories shared by my patients have provided me a broad view of human conditions in our times. But even in medicine, the role of the clinical interview is fading fast in a high throughput healthcare system, favoring diagnostic testing over detailed history taking.

Talking to people to help them talk about themselves is, fortunately, more like dance than rocket science. The sure-footed with experience can help those with less find their footing on the dance floor. The interviewer with experience can help a narrator give voice to an authentic story that arises through the dance of supportive dialogue. Unfortunately, beyond the professional sphere, there are few opportunities to develop interviewing skills—and without formal support, dancing dialogues rich in content are less likely to happen.

But, lo and behold, Voice of Witness has found that when students are provided with guidance and a supportive framework to solicit, listen to, and make sense of the stories they gather, not only do they eagerly take their partners out for a dance, they too are transformed in a variety of ways by the power of the narratives they elicit. Since we launched the educational program a few years ago, we have witnessed with regularity this student experience we have come to call transformational.

What makes the personal narrative so powerful is a matter of speculation. Oral historians and educators explain the effect as personalizing history, eliciting empathy, resonating personally, or connecting to the listener.

Having experienced this dramatic effect myself and witnessed it in others countless times, I, too, am prone to speculation. My own theory on the origins of the transformational power of firsthand accounts is quite simple: just as we are wired for language, we are also wired to relate to the raw reality of others that we are exposed to in meaningful ways. Such wiring makes sense from an evolutionary standpoint and though it may no longer confer survival advantages, we nonetheless remain susceptible to the meaningful effects of the raw ingredients of life conveyed in firsthand accounts.

In this guide, we have begun to elucidate the types of transformations that oral history can induce. They are not a matter of speculation, but rather a testament to the many transformations we have witnessed among students engaged in our programming. Looked at as a whole, these transformations provide a map of opportunity that we know will continue to expand as more teachers invite students on oral history journeys.

What kinds of stories will place students on this map of opportunity? Stories from our own backyards, our school corridors, our communities, and sometimes from those who sleep under the same roof. Often the most suitable individuals for student interviews are local people who would not commonly find themselves in the position of being asked to tell their stories. Our classroom projects are designed to outfit a classroom with all the resources needed to enable students to take local journeys into the lives of others—journeys that will often transform the way they see and think about themselves and others. Almost invariably, if the student follows through with a finished product, those interviewed are grateful for the opportunity to recount a part of their life story—and are appreciative of how students derive meaning from it. This guide will help teachers launch students on these well-defined journeys that will provide transformative experiences for students, their teachers, and those whose story they help bring to light.

THE POWER OF THE STORY

GETTING PREPARED

WHAT IS ORAL HISTORY?

The mission of Voice of Witness is "to depict human rights crises from around the world through the stories of the men and women who experience them." These stories are collected through a formal interview process, edited for length and clarity, and shaped into first-person narratives that seek to engender awareness, empathy, discussion, and advocacy. The oral history methods employed by Voice of Witness are rooted in the best practices of the Oral History Association.

According to the association, "Oral history is a field of study and a method of gathering, preserving and interpreting the voices and memories of people, communities, and participants in past events. Oral history is both the oldest type of historical inquiry, predating the written word, and one of the most modern, initiated with tape recorders in the 1940s and now using 21st-century digital technologies."

In *Doing Oral History*, Donald Ritchie explains, "An oral history interview generally consists of a well-prepared interviewer questioning an interviewee and recording their exchange in audio or video format. Recordings of the interview are transcribed, summarized, or indexed and then placed in a library or archives. These interviews may be used for research or excerpted in a publication, radio or video documentary, museum exhibition, dramatization or other form of public presentation. Recordings, transcripts, catalogs, photographs and related documentary materials can also be posted on the Internet."

Oral history is, therefore, an intentional and formal process for collecting and sharing stories that would otherwise go unheard.

WHY DO ORAL HISTORY?

Growing up in the west of Ireland, I would watch my father, a doctor, go on rounds through the countryside to visit sick families, families too poor to pay doctors' fees. My father spent long days traveling from home to home, sincerely and patiently listening to the stories of these families and administering care. Though I would often impatiently wonder when he'd be done, I gradually came to appreciate the time he gave and the sense he had of the dignity of each person.

When he returned, my father would recount the stories his patients told him. The stories were filled with suffering and sadness, yet many of them were also defined by courage and resilience in the face of great hardship... Since then my belief in the power of stories to foster compassion and guide us as a society has only grown stronger.

—Mary Robinson (from the foreword to *Nowhere to Be Home*)

Oral history can deepen students' understanding of how history is written, why it matters, and how storytelling can illuminate issues and events in a deeply personal way. By allowing themselves to be open to another's experience, students nurture their empathy and compassion; at the same time, their thinking is complicated in vital, necessary ways. Through participating in oral history, students can improve their skills as critical readers and thinkers, as they literally interact with the "text" on many levels. And doing oral history—engaging with unheard stories from outside the classroom—can strengthen both students' awareness and self-confidence.

Social justice and inclusion are the backbone of creating and sharing oral history. Oral history is usually not history from the top down, as related to us by the "great people" or the "winners" of history. It is, instead, history from the bottom up, told by individuals and communities that we rarely hear from—stories that go mostly unreported in mainstream historical narratives. Oral history expands our understanding of what is historical and who actually participates in creating history.

SUGGESTIONS FOR USING THIS GUIDE

Both parts of the guide can be used individually or can become a connected sequence that culminates with student-conducted oral histories. The lessons in the first part of the book suggest projects for the second. The lesson plans range from activities that can be done in a single class period or as five-day units, going all the way up to six-week oral history projects. In many cases, the lesson plans and narratives can be interchangeable with other narratives in the series. Our suggestions for doing so are listed with each lesson plan.

LOOKING AT HISTORY: WHO MAKES IT AND WHO WRITES IT?

TIME NEEDED: 30-45 minutes.

MATERIALS: Copies of Studs Terkel's quote and "Questions from a Worker Who Reads," a poem by Bertolt Brecht (both included below).

OBJECTIVE: To broaden students' perspectives on the sources of history.

RELATED CORE CURRICULUM STANDARDS: Speaking and Listening L.9–10.1. Reading Literature L.9–10.1, RL.9–10.2

OVERVIEW

Renowned oral historian Studs Terkel once said, "I'm celebrated for celebrating the uncelebrated." Terkel's ideas about oral history were inspired by the poem "Questions from a Worker Who Reads" by German dramatist and poet Bertolt Brecht. Using Terkel's quotation and Brecht's poem, students can begin to explore definitions of history, reconsider historical subjects, and imagine unvoiced historical narratives.

STEP ONE: Read the Studs Terkel quotation below aloud:

> You know, who built the pyramids? Ask anyone that question and they say something like 'Everybody knows who built the pyramids; it was the Pharaohs, right?' Wrong. It was the Pharaohs that had the idea of building the pyramids, for their own aggrandizement, to try to immortalize themselves…But they didn't actually build the pyramids themselves, they got peasants and slaves to do the actual work.

STEP TWO: Facilitate a brief class discussion based around student questions and responses to the quotation.

DISCUSSION QUESTIONS:

- *What is Terkel saying about the nature of history?*
- *Who decides what constitutes "history" and what does not? Why?*
- *Who is affected by those decisions?*

STEP THREE: Read the Brecht poem (as a group or silently). Address questions (terms, historical figures, etc). Use the discussion questions below as prompts for a conversation about history and how it is reported.

Who built the seven gates of Thebes?
The books are filled with names of kings.
Was it the kings who hauled the craggy blocks of stone?
And Babylon, so many times destroyed.
Who built the city up each time? In which of Lima's houses,
That city glittering with gold, lived those who built it?
In the evening when the Chinese wall was finished
Where did the masons go? Imperial Rome
Is full of arcs of triumph. Who erected them? Over whom
Did the Caesars triumph? Byzantium lives in song.
Were all her dwellings palaces? And even in Atlantis of the legend
The night the seas rushed in,
The drowning men still bawled for their slaves.

Young Alexander conquered India.
He alone?
Caesar beat the Gauls.
Was there not even a cook in his army?
Phillip of Spain wept as his fleet
was sunk and destroyed. Were there no other tears?
Frederick the Second triumphed in the Seven Years War.
Who triumphed with him?

Each page a victory.
At whose expense the victory ball?
Every ten years a great man
Who paid the piper?

So many particulars.
So many questions.

DISCUSSION QUESTIONS:

- *What does this poem suggest about silent voices?*
- *What do you imagine those people would have to say if you could go back and interview them?*
- *Who writes history? Is it biased?*
- *How would those who are not in power write the history differently?*

To help teachers explore the multiple facets and advantages of engaging oral history in the classroom, the Voice of Witness education program has developed a supportive framework for teaching and learning oral history. The framework is formatted as a Critical Thinking Diagram, allowing teachers and students to "unpack" oral history narratives and frame critical thinking and active reading questions. The Voice of Witness Framework for Oral History resonates throughout the guide and aligns with Common Core Curricular Standards (see Oral History and Core Curricular handout in Educator Resources section, page 131).

UNPACKING THE POWER OF THE STORY: THE VOICE OF WITNESS FRAMEWORK OF ORAL HISTORY

THE TRANSFORMATIONAL POWER OF STORIES

Humans learn about themselves by sharing stories. Historical narratives, creation myths, fairy tales, religious parables, trickster stories, and more are at the heart of human experience. Oral history functions in much the same way—enabling us to learn about the human condition by sharing stories. Storytelling and oral history function as "binding agents" for human contact and connection, allowing us to be transformed by the power of an individual's story.

What does this story teach us about the human condition? In what ways could this story transform one's understanding of humanity? How has this story transformed you or your understanding of the issue at hand?

AMPLIFYING UNHEARD VOICES

The Voice of Witness book series is centered on illuminating human rights crises by focusing on narratives that are unrepresented or underreported. Our education program is based on the same principle: that allowing people to speak for themselves helps give voice to the unheard stories in our own communities.

How is this voice unique? What surprising information did you learn from the voice? Why does this voice need to be amplified? Who needs to hear this voice? Why has this voice been unheard? What human rights crisis, if any, is being illuminated through this voice?

PUTTING A HUMAN FACE ON THE FACTS, FIGURES, AND STATISTICS OF HISTORY

Oral history has the capacity to "humanize history" by allowing us to see past statistics and labels to fellow humans telling stories.

How does the story humanize facts, figures, and statistics? What should one consider about the "human face" when analyzing the data?

BUILDING CRITICAL THINKING SKILLS AND NOURISHING EMPATHY AND COMPASSION

Reading and conducting oral history not only engages critical thinking skills such as interpretation, analysis, and observation, but also nourishes other crucial components of critical thinking: empathy and compassion. Oral history allows participants to emotionally connect to the stories of others—to "walk a mile in their shoes," gaining a deeply felt, nuanced understanding of the world.

How does the storyteller interpret the events of the situation, considering the facts, figures, and statistics? What discrepancies do you observe between the data of the dominant narrative and what the storyteller finds to be true? How does the narrative foster empathy for the storyteller? At what point in the story might one be moved to compassion for the storyteller? Why? How do you emotionally connect to the story?

AN OPPORTUNITY TO HONOR INDIVIDUALS

Reading or conducting oral history is an opportunity to honor a person. By conducting oral history, you accept responsibility for sharing someone's story in an accurate, respectful way. By reading someone else's story, you immediately bring that person into the room as an honored guest.

How can you best honor the narrator in creating the format of the project and in consideration of the audience? How can you best honor an individual during the interview? How did you honor the narrator during the interview and after the interview?

ILLUMINATING IDENTITY AND CULTURE

Verbal expression articulates personal and ascribed identity, a sense of place, cultural norms, and conflicts. Oral history promotes a detailed appreciation of these in a personal, relatable way.

What aspect of the storyteller's identity is illuminated in the narrative? How does the region or setting affect the storyteller? What cultural values are being highlighted? What cultural biases exist or are being broken by the story, if any? What cultural conflicts exist in the story, if any?

HISTORICAL NARRATIVE "TOOL KIT"

Oral history is a vital component in understanding the full impact of any historical or current event. It should be added to the "tool kit" of media sources, alongside traditional print media, television, internet news, textbooks, blogs, and more. Oral history provides an essential reality-based context for the world around us.

What essential reality does the story offer in helping one understand the world we live in? What does the story offer that is not a part of the Historical Narrative "Tool Kit" (media sources/news/textbooks/blogs, etc.)? What parts of the story should be contributed to the tool kit? Why?

DOING HISTORY AS OPPOSED TO JUST LEARNING ABOUT IT

In doing oral history, students are empowered with a *participatory* vision of history—a process that unfolds in front of them that they are also a part of. In learning from the oral histories of living witnesses, students can discover that history is not a predetermined set of events, but a series of choices made by individuals and groups.

In what ways does the oral history contribute to history making? How does the living witness (storyteller) illustrate that history was not a predetermined set of events? What series of choices did the individuals or groups make?

BUILDING COMMUNICATION SKILLS

Reading and studying oral history introduces students to wide-ranging and varied forms of speech, broadening vocabulary and contextual information. Through the oral history interview process, students develop their active listening skills—to "listen without judgment," gaining valuable real-world experience as trustworthy and engaged communicators. In editing and transcribing oral histories, students build their literary narrative skills, learning to edit and proofread their stories with clarity and integrity.

How did the interviewer practice empathic communication skills? How well did the questions prompt the narrator to share his or her story? What type of communication skills might be improved? What follow-up questions might be asked of the narrator? What were the most powerful moments in the interview? Why? How does the edited oral history project utilize good narrative structure compared to the original transcript of the interview?

SOCRATIC SEMINAR ON ORAL HISTORY: EXPLORING THE VOICE OF WITNESS FRAMEWORK

TIME NEEDED: One class period and one homework assignment.

MATERIALS: *Patriot Acts*, "Contracting" information from Facing History and Ourselves (page 134).

OBJECTIVE: Provide students with a discussion framework for a group exploration of the relevance and impact of oral history.

RELATED CORE CURRICULUM STANDARDS: Reading Literature RL.9–10.1, RL.11–12.1, RL.9–10.2, RL.11–12.2, RL.9–10.4, RL.11–12.4. Speaking and Listening SL.9–10.1, SL.11–12.1, SL.9–10.3, SL.11–12.3, SL.9–10.4, SL.11–12.4.

CONNECTIONS: This activity can be done with any narrative from the Voice of Witness series.

NARRATIVE EXCERPT: "The first couple of weeks after 9/11, I would say people's reactions were "polite hatred." People would see me in my *hijab* and give me the finger while I was driving. I'd be shopping, pushing the baby in the cart, and then I'd hear somebody loudly make a comment to somebody else about Afghanistan, terrorists, or whatever else.

This was totally new to me, because here we were in a lovely beach town, with our beautiful life, and you don't think that people are suddenly going to look at you like you're the enemy. That's how naïve I was." —*Rima Qamri*

STEP ONE: As homework, read Rima Qamri's narrative from *Patriot Acts* (21 pages). Encourage students to employ active reading strategies found in Educator Resource section (page 137).

STEP TWO: Explain to students that the class will be incorporating the "Contracting" framework from Facing History and Ourselves (Educator Resources section, page 134) for the day's discussion about oral history (provided that you have done the contracting exercise in a previous class). In framing the discussion, you can describe a Socratic seminar as a "collaborative, intellectual dialogue facilitated with open-ended questions about a text or issue."

STEP THREE: To get the Socratic seminar under way, begin with one or more of the following prompts from the Voice of Witness Framework for Oral History:

- *Does oral history put a "human face" on the facts, figures, and statistics of history? How?*
- *Does oral history "honor" the identity of individual narrators? If so, how?*
- *Is oral history a "legitimate" form of historical reporting? Why or why not?*
- *How do empathy and compassion relate to oral history?*
- *Can an oral history narrative be "transformative"? How can a story accomplish this?*

As the discussion unfolds, encourage students to use specific quotes from the text. Refer to the Voice of Witness Framework of Oral History as needed.

STEP FOUR: As the seminar comes to an end, resist any prescriptive or general conclusions, acknowledge the various viewpoints represented, and genuinely thank all participants.

PART 2

TAKING HISTORY PERSONALLY: VOICE OF WITNESS NARRATIVES IN THE CLASSROOM

OVERVIEW

Using narratives from the Voice of Witness book series, this section includes lesson plans, activities, and writing/discussion prompts that can bring history and contemporary issues vividly to life. Students will encounter an astonishing variety of narrators, from wrongly convicted chemist Beverly Monroe to Sudanese refugee and teacher John Mayik. The overall objective is to give teachers multiple options for introducing Voice of Witness and the power of oral history to their students.

This section is divided into different lesson plans based on contemporary issues or themes in the Voice of Witness book series: Immigration, Identity and Culture, Exile and Displacement, U.S. Justice, Security, Women's Rights, and Race, Class, and Democracy.

The section can either stand on its own, be part of a larger "issue" unit, or function as the first of a two-part oral history project that culminates in students' conducting their own oral histories. Each lesson includes suggestions for potential oral history projects as well as various media options to enhance student learning.

IMMIGRATION

OVERVIEW

The immigrant experience in the United States reflects a complex set of ideas that lend themselves to critical thinking and analysis. Using the primary source material from *Underground America: Narratives of Undocumented Lives* as a foundation, students can develop and articulate their own responses and insights into this challenging issue.

TALKING TO THE TEXT

(courtesy of Strategic Literacy Initiative)

TIME NEEDED: One to two class periods (or homework assignments).

MATERIALS: *Underground America*, sticky notes, or bookmarks. Students can also organize the activity in advance in a journal or binder.

OBJECTIVE: To divide reading content into smaller parts to help students better organize and synthesize information in an oral history narrative.

RELATED CORE CURRICULUM STANDARDS: Reading History RH.9–10.2, RH.9–10.3, RH.9–10.4.

CONNECTIONS: This activity can be done with any narrative from the Voice of Witness series.

NARRATIVE EXCERPT: "It wasn't long after I got married the second time that a church from Houston sent a letter to my pastor in the Eastern Cape. The American church was asking our church for missionaries to volunteer. My pastor's wife called me that Saturday. She said, 'There's a church in the USA that needs a missionary. Are you still interested in going to America?' I said yes right away because—to tell the truth—I have a lot of debt at home. And, you know, we have the idea that everything in America is perfect because that's what we see on TV and in the movies. In America, you find dollars lying in the grass, every leaf on a tree is a dollar. Right now, if you call somebody in South Africa and say, 'Do you want to come to America, even if it's to wash my pig?' I promise you that that person will say, 'Oh yes, please let me come and wash your pig!' People will do anything to get here, to make money to send home. So, even though missionaries don't get paid, I was sure people in America would help me." —*Liso*

STEP ONE: Use the chart on the following page to help students organize their thoughts as they read Liso's narrative (18 pp) from *Underground America* (30 minutes).

STEP TWO: Students work in small groups and share their results from the activity. They should compare questions and predictions and make connections to other related readings and their own lives (10–12 minutes).

STEP THREE (optional): If desired, questions, predictions, and connections can become the basis for student personal essays.

POSSIBLE ORAL HISTORY PROJECT: Class creates an oral history project focusing on moments of change or how specific choices have impacted their lives.

MEDIA OPTION: African Voices Podcast
African Voices (*www.africansinchicago.org/africanvoices*) is the official podcast of the United African Organization, a coalition of African national associations that promotes social and economic justice, civic participation, and empowerment of African immigrants and refugees in Chicago.

TALK TO THE TEXT

DIRECTIONS

CHUNK IT!: Break the text into bite-size pieces, e.g., a paragraph or two that you can read easily.

READ: Read the text to yourself one time first.

TALK TO THE TEXT: Think about any questions, predictions, or connections (to things you already know) you have with the text. Mark these right on the text itself, or on sticky notes if you are reading from a book.

REPEAT: Keep reading and Talking to the Text with the next chunks.

METACOGNITIVE REFLECTIONS	
I *think/believe/wonder*…	This *reminds* me of…
I'm *confused* about…	I'll *reread*…
I can *picture*…	I *predict* that…
This is *like*…	

EXAMINING THE MYTHS
AND FACTS OF IMMIGRATION

TIME NEEDED: One class period and one homework session, or two class periods.

MATERIALS: *Underground America*, the American Civil Liberties Union's *Myths and Facts About Immigration* (2008), large pieces of butcher paper or large (poster-size) sticky notes, markers.

OBJECTIVE: Through reading, analysis, and discussion, students enhance their understanding of U.S. immigration issues.

RELATED CORE CURRICULAR STANDARDS: Reading Literature RL.9–10.1. Reading History RH.9–10.1, RL.9–10.2. Speaking and Listening SL.9–10.1, SL.9–10.3, SL.9–10.4.

CONNECTIONS: Lesson can also be used with the following narratives from *Patriot Acts:* Rana Sodhi, Usma Naheed Abbasi, Anser Mehmood, Farid Rodriguez; *Out of Exile:* Panther Alier, Abuk Bak Macham; *Nowhere to Be Home:* Law Eh Soe, U Agga Nya Na.

ESSENTIAL QUESTION:

- *How do the stories from* Underground America *complicate your thinking about immigration issues?*

NARRATIVE EXCERPT: "The day before the hurricane arrived, I went to work at the casino as usual. That day the management made us work like never before. We cleaned absolutely everything, working extra hours. People were saying that Katrina was coming but I wasn't sure what it was. Where I'm from we'd never heard of hurricanes.

Everyone on the overnight cleaning crew was Hispanic. There were Americans who worked the night shift, too, but my American coworkers didn't clean. They did other jobs, like security and food service. That day, some of them said to me, 'Diana, what are you still doing here cleaning? Let's go! Katrina's coming!' But everyone on cleaning crew had been told by the supervisor to stay longer than our usual hours that night, that there was going to be an inspection the next day. Everyone else was leaving. They left us there to go on working: cleaning and cleaning." —*Diana*

PREPARATION: Download and photocopy *Immigration Myths and Facts* from the ACLU's Immigrants' Rights Project for students (*www.aclu.org/immigrants-rights/immigration-myths-and-facts*). Create reading groups for nine of the narratives from *Underground America* (to correspond to the nine myths/facts of immigration), using the following narratives: Diana (12 pp.), Mr. Lai (20 pp.), Roberto (19 pp.), Liso (18 pp.), Lorena (20 pp.), Jose Garcia (17 pp.), Farid (18 pp.), Edela (19 pp.), and Estrella (16 pp.). Other narratives from the book can be substituted for the ones listed above.

STEP ONE: Hand out copies of *Immigration Facts and Myths* to be read during class or as homework (20 minutes).

STEP TWO: Assign each group one of the nine selected narratives from *Underground America*. Groups can read their narratives silently, aloud during class, or they can be assigned as homework. While students are reading their assigned narratives, they should copy three to six direct quotes from their narrators that seem to *align* with or *contradict* the nine myths and facts of immigration (45 minutes).

STEP THREE: Groups should be given time to discuss individual quotes. Each group should assign a facilitator and should be prepared to discuss the following (10–15 minutes):

- *Why quotes were chosen and how they specifically connect to particular myths and realities of immigration.*
- *How chosen quotes helped students empathize with the personal experiences of the narrators.*
- *How chosen quotes enhanced students' understanding of immigration issues.*

STEP THREE: On nine poster-size sticky notes or large pieces of butcher paper, write each immigration myth at the top and the fact at the bottom. Hang them up in various places around the room. Have several pens placed near each "station." Give students time to move around the room, writing their chosen quotes directly on the particular myth/reality of immigration that it relates to (15 minutes).

STEP FOUR: Class silently examines the quotes at each station (5–7 minutes).

STEP FIVE: CIRCLE OF VOICES: Students return to their narrative groups. Using three minutes of silent time, each group considers their responses and reactions to what they have just viewed at each myth/fact station. Each group member then has three minutes of uninterrupted time to discuss his or her responses, reactions and questions. Then, members may react to the comments that have been expressed (15–20 minutes).

STEP 6 (optional): Using the Circle of Voices format, have groups consider the following questions (courtesy of Teaching Tolerance):

- *Where do you think these myths come from?*
- *Who benefits from these myths?*
- *Why are these myths untrue?*

POSSIBLE ORAL HISTORY PROJECT: Using quotes from the narratives and responses during the Circle of Voices activity, students can craft potential interview questions for an oral history project focusing on immigration issues.

MEDIA OPTION: Use **Wordle** (*www.wordle.net*) or **Tagxedo** (*www.tagxedo.com*) to create "word clouds," which are visual representations of words that appear in a text. Words or phrases that are used more frequently appear larger. Class could create an additional representation of the myths and facts of immigration.

ORAL HISTORY/AMERICAN DREAM "POSITION PAPER"

TIME NEEDED: One to two class periods and two to three homework sessions

MATERIALS: *Underground America*, butcher paper or poster-size sticky notes, pens, paper (student journals), and computer.

OBJECTIVE: Use critical thinking, writing, and analytical skills to convey understanding of immigration issues through first-person narratives.

RELATED CORE CURRICULUM STANDARDS: Reading Informational Texts RI.9–10.1, RI.11–12.1, RI.9–10.2, RI.11–12.2, RI.9–10.3, RI.11–12.3. Writing W.9–10.1, W.11–12.1, W.9–10.2, W.11–12.2.

CONNECTIONS: Lesson can also be used with the following narratives from *Patriot Acts*: Rana Sodhi, Usma Naheed Abbasi, Anser Mehmood, Farid Rodriguez; *Out of Exile*: Panther Alier, Abuk Bak Macham; *Nowhere to Be Home*: Law Eh Soe, U Agga Nya Na.

ESSENTIAL QUESTION:

- *To what extent is the American Dream a reality for immigrants?*

NARRATIVE EXCERPT: "The feeling that I had to find a way out for myself and my family grew stronger and stronger over the next few years. We just couldn't go on like this. This was no way to live. And I had so much anger toward the government that I really got to thinking, if I didn't get out then I'd probably just end up in jail. I just had no faith in China. I didn't know how I was going to do it, but I knew I had to go to America." —*Mr. Lai*

OVERVIEW

This lesson can serve as a basic introduction to position papers, giving students an opportunity to practice their critical thinking and writing skills.

DAY ONE

STEP ONE: Students respond to the following prompt in their journals or binders (10 minutes):

- *What is the American Dream?*

STEP TWO: Write the words "American Dream" on the board and have students share out the responses from their journals, while capturing their ideas on the board so everyone can see them. (*5–7 minutes*)

STEP THREE: Based on student responses on the board, and from a brief analysis of the economic, cultural and political factors of immigration, class comes up with a working definition of "American Dream" (20–25 minutes). To aid in student analysis, have a class reading/brief discussion using the *Immigration Myths and Facts* from the ACLU's Immigrants' Rights Project.

Have students discuss the myriad factors that determine their responses. Students may also reflect on differing family experiences, for either first-generation Americans or families that have been in the United States for generations.

As an additional analysis tool, students may wish to explore the National Archives (*www.archives.gov*) for speeches by U.S. presidents and members of Congress that reference the American Dream. This may provide meaningful context regarding national political definitions of the term.

STEP 4: Introduce *Underground America* and assign the following narratives: Jose Garcia (17 pp.), Elizabeth (18 pp.), and Mr. Lai (20 pp.). Use most of the remainder of the class period for students to begin their reading. The rest can be done as homework and/or during the following class period. Encourage students to use active reading strategies (10–15 minutes).

STEP FOUR: Before the end of class, write the class definition of American Dream on a large piece of butcher paper or poster-size sticky note and hang it in an accessible location in the room. During the remainder of the unit, students will write comments, quotations, and questions related to their reading on this poster. What they write can help shape their ideas for their position paper (2 minutes).

DAY TWO

STEP ONE: If needed, give students additional time to finish their reading (15 minutes).

STEP TWO: Allow the class some time to write on the American Dream poster (5–7 minutes).

STEP THREE: Give students the Position Paper handout, discussing the format and answering any questions about the assignment. The goal in introducing the assignment is to encourage students to think deeply about their topic/writing and not to get too bogged down by format (15 minutes).

POSITION PAPER

"Good thinking is good writing."

WHAT IS A POSITION PAPER?

A position paper is a relatively short piece of writing that communicates your understanding of an assigned text. The goal is for you to put forth a clear and organized essay of your thoughts, rather than writing a summary of what you read.

THE ASSIGNMENT: For your assignment, you must take a position on the following question:

To what extent is the American Dream a reality for immigrants?
Your evidence should come from the assigned narratives from *Underground America*. You may also use information and ideas from the American Dream poster. Your position paper should be no more than **two typed pages** (double-spaced), incorporating the following format:

I. INTRODUCTION:

Introduce the issue and provide background. The introduction should include your definition of the American Dream (which can differ from the class definition). As with other essays, your thesis should be the last sentence of your introductory paragraph.

II. BODY:

Assert your first claim, providing textual evidence or proof (but please do not fill your entire paper with quotes). Explain how your evidence or proof supports your claim. You should strive to make three claims with proofs and explanations.

III. CONCLUSION:

Restate the strongest points of your argument and provide a "plan of action" for addressing the issues presented. *Sample question*: What needs to change in American society for the American Dream to be realistic?

THE PROCESS:

Over the course of several days, here is how you should develop your position paper:

1. *Thesis and outline*
2. *Work on rough draft*
3. *Revise draft*
4. *Work on final draft*
5. *Turn in final draft*

STEP FOUR: Have a brief discussion about student responses to the reading. Ask students if they can connect any quotes to their definition of American Dream (5–7 minutes).

STEP FIVE: Students may find it helpful to have a class brainstorm session for creating a strong thesis sentence. For this brainstorm session, pose the following questions (10 minutes):

- *Does my thesis sentence attempt to answer or explore a challenging question?*
- *Does my thesis sentence inspire other points of view?*
- *Is my thesis sentence too general or vague? Should I focus on some more specific aspect of my topic?*

STEP SIX: Any remaining class time should be used for students to create drafts of a thesis sentence followed by a basic outline of their paper. If desired, students can work in small groups to develop their ideas. For homework, students should finish their outlines and begin working on their rough drafts.

DAY THREE

STEP ONE: As a warm-up activity, students should work in groups of three and share their thesis sentences and any quotes from the narratives that back up their thesis. Encourage them to refer back to the previous day's questions about thesis sentences and to the American Dream definition (7–10 minutes).

STEP TWO: Address any questions regarding thesis sentences, outlines, quotes, etc. (5 minutes).

STEP THREE: Create a class "writing lab," allowing students to work on their position papers. Offer assistance and ideas as needed (25–30 minutes).

STEP FOUR: Before the end of the class period, allow students to write on the American Dream poster (5 minutes). For homework, students should revise and finish their final drafts.

STEP ONE: Select two opposing student position papers to be read or presented to the class (students can also create two groups based on similar positions). Create an informal class debate about immigration issues. Class can also do a "fishbowl" discussion.* Refer to **Contracting** or class agreements if necessary (30 minutes). In conclusion, pose the following questions to the class:

- *How has this process "complicated" your thinking about immigration issues?*
- *What quote from* Underground America *inspired your position most?*
- *Did your definition of American Dream change during the process? If so, how?*

POSSIBLE ORAL HISTORY PROJECT: Create an oral history project focusing on different aspects of the American Dream. Potential interview questions could include:

- *What does it mean to be an American?*
- *Who gets to be an American?*
- *What is the American Dream?*
- *How does the American Dream compare to American realities?*

MEDIA OPTION: Organizational websites:

67 Sueños: A youth-led collective based in San Francisco that strives to tell the stories of everyday young people who are often left out of the national narrative on immigration reform. (*www.67suenos.org*)

Define American: Define American brings new voices into the immigration conversation, shining a light on a growing twenty-first century underground railroad: American citizens who are forced to fill in where our immigration system fails. (*www.defineamerican.com*)

---

* A fishbowl is a teaching strategy that encourages students to both contribute to the discussion and be active listeners. It requires a small circle of 6-8 chairs (or however many would best suit your classroom needs) to create the inner "fishbowl," and an outer ring of students sitting or standing around the inner circle. The students in the inner circle, or "fishbowl," take turns responding to a prompt or discussion topic while the students in the outer circle listen. After a designated amount of time (typically 10-15 minutes), the inner and outer circles switch. Fishbowls can be particularly effective for challenging or difficult discussion topics.

IDENTITY AND CULTURE

OVERVIEW

This section will enable students to explore identity and culture through the personalizing experience of reading oral history. The lessons in this section can be used for examining personal and national identity as well as for gaining new perspectives on global culture. The suggested narratives from the Voice of Witness series can serve as strong "connecting points" for students to see aspects of their own experience reflected in the lives of the narrators.

THE IDENTITY BOX

TIME NEEDED: One homework session and one or two class periods.

MATERIALS: *Patriot Acts*, a small cardboard or paper box, various craft supplies (scissors, glue, fabric, colored pens or pencils), and various easy-to-find household objects.

OBJECTIVE: To analyze and interpret identity through oral history and a personalized art project.

RELATED CORE CURRICULUM STANDARDS: Reading History RH.9–10.1, RH.9–10.4. Speaking and Listening SL.9–10.1.

CONNECTIONS: This activity can be done with any narrative from the Voice of Witness series.

NARRATIVE EXCERPT: "My parents were from Polish-German descent. I grew up in Toledo, Ohio, in a close, tight-knit family with three sisters and a brother. My given name is Edward, but my family started calling me Zachary, my grandfather's name, because my dad, my uncle, and his son were all called Edward!

I met my second wife after I had converted to Islam. She told me that the name Zakariya exists in Arabic. I said that was perfect, and so I changed my name legally to Zakariya. I also changed my middle name to Muhammad. I wanted an attachment to the religion, and for people to know who I am, maybe in a more subtle way. When I changed my name, and people at work asked me what they should call me, I'd say, 'you can still call me Ed,' whatever they were comfortable with, because they'd known me as Edward for so long. But everyone else is to call me by my chosen name." —*Zak Muhammad Reed*

STEP ONE: Have the students create an Identity Worksheet. On a piece of paper, they should draw two columns: one with the heading Ascribed Identity and the other with the heading Personal Identity. Ascribed Identity describes how the world sees someone and Personal Identity describes how that person sees him or her self (2 minutes).

STEP TWO: Students read Gurwinder Singh (11 pp.), Hani Khan (5 pp.), or Zak Muhammad Reed's narrative (13 pp.) from *Patriot Acts*. As they read, instruct them to write down all quotes or references to the narrator's ascribed and personal identity on their Identity Worksheet (30 minutes).

STEP THREE: Using the Identity Worksheet as a resource, have students decorate their small cardboard or paper boxes to reflect the ascribed and personal identity of the narrator. The outside of the box will contain words, images, symbols, and drawings that reflect the narrator's ascribed identity, and the inside of the box will contain objects, images, quotations, and individual words that reflect the narrator's personal identity. Objects and other items for the box should be items easily found at home or in the classroom. To create personal connections, students should then create a second identity box, using themselves as subjects (40 minutes).

STEP FOUR: Class divides into three groups (according to the narratives they read). Groups present the contents of both of their identity boxes. During their presentations, they should be prepared to discuss the following (35 minutes):

- *How their chosen quotes, images, and objects relate to the identity of their narrators.*
- *How specific textual examples illuminate and explain their choices.*
- *Specific ways in which the project helped them explore the concept of identity and what connections they made to their own lives.*
- *How the project enabled them to personally connect with various aspects of the narrator's identity.*

POSSIBLE ORAL HISTORY PROJECT: Students create an oral history project based on personal and ascribed identity by interviewing classmates, faculty, administrators, and staff. This can also be done with family and community members outside of school.

MEDIA OPTION: If desired, students can create online versions of the Identity Box in the form of a website, PowerPoint presentation, or a short digital video.

LITERATURE CIRCLE: IDENTITY AND ZIMBABWE'S LAND REFORM

TIME NEEDED: Five class periods (several can be done as homework if desired).

MATERIALS: *Hope Deferred,* Timeline of Zimbabwe (p. 467) Glossary (p. 462), and Political Violence, the War Veterans, and the Land Invasions (p. 476); the Literature Circle Handout, the *New York Times* online Country Profile on Zimbabwe, (*topics.nytimes.com/top/news/international/ countriesandterritories/zimbabwe/index.html?scp=1&sq=zimbabwe%20country%20profile&st=cs*), magazines, newspapers, poster board, and glue sticks/tape.

OBJECTIVE: Use oral history, literary analysis, and research to examine the role of national identity in connection with Zimbabwe's land reform policies.

RELATED CORE CURRICULUM STANDARDS: Reading History RH.9–10.1, RH.11–12.1, RH.9–10.2, RH.11–12.2, RH.9–10.6, RH.11–12.6, RH.9–10.9, RH.11–12.9. Writing W.9–10.1, W.11–12.1, W.9–10.2, W.11–12.2, W.9–10.7, W.11–12.7. Speaking and Listening SL.9–10.1, SL.11–12.1, SL.9–10.4, SL.11–12.4.

CONNECTIONS: Literature Circle activity can be used with any narrative in the Voice of Witness series.

ESSENTIAL QUESTIONS:

- *How does Zimbabwean national identity influence ownership rights to the farmland of Zimbabwe?*
- *Who is a "true" Zimbabwean and who has the rights to Zimbabwe's farmland?*
- *How has colonial history complicated the issue?*

NARRATIVE EXCERPT: "Other farmers in the area harvested their tobacco and maize and then left. They were not sure if they were safe from having their land invaded, with violence. A while after I harvested, I was left alone there, still thinking that I was safe. I thought this pressure to give up our land was short term and would not last. I also had some crops in the ground, so I had to stay longer than everybody else. If you go into farming, you put all your money in the soil, and then it's only when it grows that you can see it. There was no way I would just uproot and quit.

I tried to appeal through Zanu-PF [the ruling political party] structures. Blacks were supposed to benefit from this land invasion—that's what I heard. I thought I was black enough! All I needed was to make a claim and I would keep this piece of land." —*Tsitsi*

OVERVIEW

Zimbabwe's recent history entails a detailed system of farm and land ownership, which includes primarily white-owned commercial farms and many designated "rural area" farms, which fall under the jurisdiction of tribal chiefs. In 2000, Robert Mugabe's Zanu-PF government instituted a policy of land reform and began taking over predominately white-owned farms and redistributing them to war veterans and other black Zimbabweans.

PREPARATION: Zimbabwe's land distribution policy exacerbated questions of national identity: who is a "true" Zimbabwean and who has the rights to Zimbabwe's farmland? Class should become familiar with contextualizing information about the history of Zimbabwe and land reform in the country. Create several student "research groups" to provide background information in the following categories:

- *Economics*
- *Politics*
- *Agriculture*
- *Colonialism*

Maps, posters, articles, quotes and images will all provide a historical snapshot of Zimbabwe and will reflect the various identities of its people (one class, one homework session).

STEP ONE: Groups present their research to the class. After each group concludes its presentation, discuss the following questions (15 minutes):

- *How does this information create a "narrative" or story about Zimbabwe?*
- *If you had to relate this information as a story, how would you tell it?*

STEP TWO: Create groups of four students and assign each group the following narratives from *Hope Deferred*: Nicola (15 pp.), Tsitsi (18 pp.), Briggs (31 pp.), and George (26 pp.). Give each student a copy of the Literature Circle handout. Read through the instructions together. **Note:** The activities related to the Literature Circle can be completed during or outside class (15 minutes).

STEP THREE: At the conclusion of their fourth meeting, groups should decide how they would like to "present" their Literature Circle findings to the rest of the class. Part of this process is making choices about which Literature Circle job each member of the group will be responsible for presenting (10 minutes).

STEP FOUR: Incorporating their chosen vocabulary words, passages, connectors, illustrations, etc., groups will create posters (digital if available or desired) that feature the work done in their Literature Circles. In addition to the information they have already gathered, encourage them to "fill in" their presentations with images cut out of magazines, maps, and whatever else they feel communicates their responses to the narratives. Can be done during class or as a group homework assignment (60–70 minutes).

STEP FIVE: Each Literature Circle presents to the class. Presentations should be about five to seven minutes each and incorporate time for comments and questions. Reflecting back on the discussion questions of the unit may be useful, as well as considering the following (50-60 minutes):

- *Have any of the "connectors" touched on local issues? If so, what are the similarities and differences to issues in Zimbabwe?*
- *Have groups chosen similar passages or quotes? If so, how do they reflect the particular identity of the narrators?*
- *Is there a fair way to resolve the land reform issue in Zimbabwe? What do you predict for the future of the country?*

POSSIBLE ORAL HISTORY PROJECT: Class creates an oral history project focusing on local examples of potentially unjust policies or laws, and the complicated, personal struggles that result from them.

MEDIA OPTION: Documentary Film: *Banished* (dir. Marco Williams). Center for Investigative Reporting/Two Tone Productions/CPB, 2007: A hundred years ago, in communities across the United States, white residents forced thousands of black families to flee their homes. *Banished* tells the story of three of these communities and their black descendants, who return to learn their histories. The film contemplates questions of privilege, responsibility, denial, healing, reparations, and identity. (*www.pbs.org/independentlens/banished/film.html*)

THE LITERATURE CIRCLE

Each member of the group will read the four assigned narratives from *Hope Deferred*. For each narrative, one member of the group will take on one of the jobs mentioned below. While you read your narratives, you will be responsible for completing the tasks described below.

Groups will get together on four separate occasions (in or out of class), and each member will contribute what their individual job requires. Remember to save group work! It will be used to create a presentation for the rest of the class.

DISCUSSION DIRECTOR: Your job is to write a list of questions that your group might want to discuss about today's reading. Don't worry about small details; *your task is to help people talk over the big ideas and share reactions.* Usually the best discussion questions come from your own thoughts, feelings, and concerns as you read. Or you can use some of the general questions suggested to develop topics for group discussions: *Did anything surprise you? What are the most important ideas in the reading? What do you predict will happen next?* You are the person who begins the group discussion. You ask questions…get responses from ALL members…ask a question…get responses…etc.

PASSAGE MASTER/VOCABULARY BUILDER: Your job is to locate at least *five* special sections or quotations from the reading that the group should examine. You want to help people notice the most interesting, funny, puzzling, and important sections of the text. You decide and identify which passages or paragraphs (note the page number) are worth reviewing and then write plans for how they should be shared with the group. Write down why you think the passage is significant or should be discussed. You can read passages aloud yourself, ask someone else to read, or have the group read them silently, then discuss. Then you will share why you selected the passage and what it means to you. As Vocabulary Builder, your job is to be on the lookout for at least *five* important words—new, interesting, strange, important, puzzling, or unfamiliar words—words that members of the group need to notice to understand. Mark some of the key words while you are reading, then write them down in the context of the sentence. Discuss these words with your group and why the meaning of each word is important.

ILLUSTRATOR: Your job is to draw some kind of picture related to the reading. It can be a sketch, cartoon, storyboard, diagram, flowchart, magazine cutouts, etc. You can draw a picture of something that is discussed specifically in the text, something that the reading reminded you of, or something that conveys any idea or feeling you got from the reading. Any sort of drawing or graphic representation is okay—you can even label parts of the drawing if it helps. During the Literature Circle discussion, show your picture and explain how it shows your interpretation and understanding of the text or part of the text.

CONNECTOR: Your job is to find connections between the material your group is reading and the world outside. This means connecting the reading to your own life or personal observations, to happenings at school or in the community, to similar events at other times and places, to other people or problems that you are reminded of, to other pieces of literature or films you have seen. Any connection you make with the book is fine. Explain in writing your connections and be prepared to share them with your group.

YOUTH STORIES FROM BURMA: A "LIVING SCULPTURE" ACTIVITY

TIME NEEDED: Two to three class periods and one homework session.

MATERIALS: *Nowhere to Be Home*, journals or notebooks, Living Sculptures handout, the *New York Times* online Myanmar (Burma) Country Profile (*http://topics.nytimes.com/top/news/international/countriesandterritories/myanmar/index.html*), Human Rights Watch: World Report Burma (*www.hrw.org/world-report-2011/burma*).

OBJECTIVE: To bring oral histories to life in order to better understand and connect with the lives of youth in Burma.

RELATED CORE CURRICULUM STANDARDS: Reading History RH.9–10.1, RH.9–10.5, RH.9–10.7, Writing, W.9–10.3, W.11–12.3, Speaking and Listening SL.9–10.1, SL.9–10.2.

CONNECTIONS: This activity can be done with any set of narratives from the Voice of Witness series.

OVERVIEW

Borrowing techniques from theater arts training, this lesson will enable students to develop their empathy skills through direct physical and emotional engagement with several youth narrators from *Nowhere to Be Home*. Through collaborative group work and analysis, students will engage with the stories of young people living in a police state, allowing them to experience "walking a mile in someone else's shoes."

ESSENTIAL QUESTIONS:

- *How can I use my body, voice, and emotions to "read between the lines" of history?*
- *How can I use my own interpretations and experience to connect with the lives of the book's narrators?*
- *How can I connect the realities of a police state with my own life, community, and country?*

NARRATIVE EXCERPT: "There was a special door for prisoners to walk through, and it was very hard for us because we had to kneel down when we walked.

After that we had to take off our hoods, and I saw that it was all females in the room with me. I was the youngest. Everybody knew each other from working in politics, and they said, 'Don't cry, don't be afraid. We can go back home one day. They can't do anything to us, we will take care of each other.' There were some old people, like sixty-five- and eighty-year-old women in our group.

I felt sorry for my father when I was at the prison, because they wrote my family name on a piece of paper that I had to hold when they took my prisoner photo—one photo from the front, and one from the side. I thought, *I am the daughter in prison*. But I hoped maybe my father would still be proud of me.

After that, they put me directly in a cell. It was in a special place, usually for people with a death sentence or for people who break the prison rules—solitary confinement." —*Mau Su Mon*

TEACHER PREPARATION: Take some time to become familiar with recent Burmese (Myanmar) history. Among other sources, the *New York Times* Country Profile of Myanmar is a good place to start (especially as it is constantly updated). *Human Rights Watch: World Report Burma* is another good (and updated) resource. This information should be compiled into a one-page Burma Fact Sheet for students.

DAY ONE

STEP ONE: Hand out Burma Fact Sheet. Present an overview of Burmese history, focusing on the period of the military coup (1962) up to the present. Provide details as to what defines a police state and specifically how it may affect the lives of youth (15 minutes).

STEP TWO: Introduce *Nowhere to Be Home* and break students into cooperative learning groups of four. Each group will read one of the following four narratives: Byin Pu (26 pp.), Mau Su Mon (28 pp.), Khine Kyaw (18 pp.), and Hla Min (15 pp.). Allow time for groups to begin reading their narratives aloud to each other. Encourage them to employ active reading strategies. The remainder of the reading should be done as homework or at the beginning of the next class period (25–30 minutes).

STEP THREE: Share the Living Sculptures and Inner Monologue handouts. Introduce the activity by announcing that groups will be "walking a mile in their narrators' shoes." They will be reenacting pivotal moments from their narrators' lives by creating a series of "living sculptures." Providing a definition of "empathy" may be useful (see discussion questions). If needed, show examples of sculptures to help students visualize the activity. Also introduce the Inner Monologue activity and definition. If needed, provide literary or film/video examples of inner monologue or "subtext" (10–12 minutes).

LIVING SCULPTURES AND INNER MONOLOGUE

CREATING YOUR SCULPTURES

Each group will create *four* sculptures that represent four important moments from the story of your narrator. They should be "impactful" moments in their story. Each sculpture needs to relate to a short selection from the narrative (no longer than a paragraph). Everyone in the group needs to be in each sculpture. One person in each sculpture needs to represent the narrator—make sure you trade off!

Sculptures can represent moments from your narrator's life in many ways—you can represent or "show" what is happening in the moment with other "characters" in the narrator's story, or you can create sculptures that represent the narrator's emotions or feelings. You can also create visual symbols and metaphors—the possibilities are endless!

QUOTE FROM NARRATIVE

Once your group has arranged itself into each of your sculptures (four total), one member of the group will briefly step out of the sculpture to read the selection from the narrative that inspired the sculpture. When he or she is done, he or she should step back into the sculpture. You will repeat this for each sculpture.

INNER MONOLOGUE

Inner monologue is a term that describes the "voice" in each of our heads that represents the thoughts and feelings we have but do not say. If our "outer monologue" is what we choose to express out loud, then our inner monologue is the powerful stream of information we choose to keep to ourselves.

During each of your sculptures, whoever is portraying the narrator will *step out* of the sculpture and read a prepared inner monologue that begins with the phrase *"Sometimes I feel…"* This inner monologue or speech should be no longer than a paragraph and should relate to the quote that the sculpture represents. Think about what your narrator is *feeling* but not *saying* and use it for your inner monologue. Whoever represents the narrator in each sculpture should write the inner monologue.

RUNNING ORDER FOR SCULPTURES

1. Sculpture One (held throughout sequence).
2. Quote from Narrative
3. Inner Monologue ("Sometimes I feel…")

Repeat this sequence four times. Each sculpture/reading should take about sixty seconds.

DAY TWO

STEP ONE: If needed, allow time for students to finish reading narratives (7–10 minutes).

STEP TWO: Answer any questions about the activity—living sculptures, supporting text, inner monologue, "sometimes I feel," etc. (5 minutes).

STEP THREE: Students get into their groups and put together their four living sculptures, which include supporting quotes for each sculpture and an inner monologue paragraph ("Sometimes I feel"). Groups will need consensus about the four "impactful" moments as well as the physical composition of each sculpture. Each group member will also need time to compose his or her inner monologue for the sculpture in which he or she represents the narrator (30–35 minutes). During this work session, the following prompts or "side-coaching" may be helpful:

- *What are the details of your quote? How can you physically tell the "story" behind the quote?*
- *Allow your entire bodies to be expressive!*
- *You may find it helpful to write the "Sometimes I feel" paragraph after you have created each sculpture. Your body language will give you ideas about what your narrator is feeling.*
- *Make sure you "rehearse" all four sculptures, quotes, and inner monologues several times. It is a great way to check your work.*

DAY THREE

STEP ONE: If desired, give groups time to do a final "rehearsal" before their presentations (7–10 minutes).

STEP TWO: Groups present their sculptures. Sculptures should be presented in chronological order of the narrative. Some students may be testing their comfort zones, so remind everyone about any "class agreements" that are used (*30-35 minutes*).

STEP THREE: After each group has presented their sculptures, facilitate a debrief/class discussion that enables students to respond to the activity. It may be useful to begin with each group describing their experience (10–15 minutes). *Note that this step can also be done as a combination journal writing/ discussion activity.*

DISCUSSION QUESTIONS:

- *Did creating physical sculptures to represent your narrator's experience allow you to better understand his or her life in Burma? How?*
- *The dictionary definition of* empathy *is "being aware of, and sharing another person's feelings, experiences, and emotions." Did this activity enable you to do that? If so, how?*
- *What personal connections did you make with your narrators? Do aspects of their experience resonate with you?*
- *"Police state" is a basic term that describes a complex situation. How can you apply the term outside of Burma? Can you find any parallels in the community? In the United States?*

POSSIBLE ORAL HISTORY PROJECT: Class creates an oral history project exploring local policies or laws, examining the complications and sometimes unintended consequences resulting from them.

MEDIA OPTION: Video: *Words of Kyaw Zwar* (dir. Takaaki Okada). Short video of narrator featured in *Nowhere to Be Home*: *www.vimeo.com/30103194*

Organizational website: **Albany Park Theater Project** (APTP). APTP creates original theater that shares the real-life stories of urban teens, immigrants, and working-class Americans. APTP humanizes issues that impact real people but too often get discussed as abstract concepts. (*www.aptpchicago.org*)

EXILE
AND DISPLACEMENT

OVERVIEW

This section explores the cultural, political, and emotional realities of being forced from one's home or country of origin. It allows teachers and students to contemplate definitions of "home" as they personalize the plight of narrators who carry "home" on their backs or in their hearts. The narratives in *Out of Exile*, *Throwing Stones at the Moon*, and *Refugee Hotel* create an opportunity for a personal and nuanced exploration of displacement, resettlement, and the assumptions that come with the labels Exile, Refugee, and Internally Displaced Person.

EXAMINING THE LABELS "REFUGEE" AND "EXILE" THROUGH STORYBOARDS

———————

TIME NEEDED: Three class periods and two homework sessions.

MATERIALS: *Out of Exile*, the *New York Times* Sudan Profile (*topics.nytimes.com/top/news/international/ countriesandterritories/sudan/index.htm*), Storyboards handout (on page 48), colored pencils and pencils, magazines, and definitions of *refugee* and *exile*.

OBJECTIVE: Through literary analysis and visual storytelling, students increase understanding about exiles and refugees while exploring the power of labels.

RELATED CORE CURRICULUM STANDARDS: Reading History RH.9–10.1, RH.9–10.2. Speaking and Listening L.9–10.1, SL.11–12.1. Writing W.9–10.1, W.11–12.1.

CONNECTIONS: Other Voice of Witness narratives that can be used for this lesson: Abuk Bak Macham, Panther Alier from *Out of Exile*; Law Eh Soe and Khine Kyaw from *Nowhere to Be Home;* and Farid from *Underground America*.

OVERVIEW

This lesson allows students to personalize the realities of being an exile or refugee as they explore the power of labels. Using narratives from *Out of Exile* and utilizing a storyboard technique to summarize their responses, students will creatively express the challenges of individuals who have been removed from their homes and separated from their families.

ESSENTIAL QUESTIONS:

- *What is it like to have to leave your home, family, and country?*
- *What challenges (internal and external) does an exiled person or refugee face?*
- *What stereotypes exist around refugees and exiles?*
- *How can you summarize your responses using a storyboard?*
- *What connections can you make to this issue from U.S. history?*

NARRATIVE EXCERPT: "The children come to school, and we feed them a meal every day now. They are happy students, and they do very well. They read very well. They do very well on the national exams every year—better than the national average. They like being at Sud Academy, because Sudanese often get harassed in the Kenyan schools—their classmates will come up to them, poke them, say, 'Hey! You are a refugee. You create problems in your country and now you want to come here to make trouble for us.'

"The kids will wonder, 'What is a refugee?' because most of the young ones were born here in Nairobi. They'll come home to their parents at night and ask about this word. And that's not a good way to find out." —*John Mayik*

WHAT I KNOW	WHAT I *WANT* TO KNOW	WHAT I *LEARNED*

STEP ONE: Use the KWL chart format on the previous page to begin a student journal activity and discussion about their understanding of the labels *refugee* and *exile*. (5–7 minutes) The "W" (what I learned), should be addressed at the end of each class period or the end of the unit. A large version of the chart should be easily accessible to students in order for them to post responses and questions throughout the lesson.

STEP TWO: Share the following definitions/explanations with the class and discuss them in relationship to the KWL activity (5–7 minutes).

Refugee: Refugees are persons who have fled their homes and cannot return because they fear their life is in danger. People become refugees when one or more of their basic human rights are violated or threatened.

Exile: Exile is being forced to leave one's country or home. Voluntary exile is the departure from one's country due to political strife or dissension.

STEP THREE: Use the *New York Times* Country Profile to briefly introduce Sudanese history and *Out of Exile* (15 minutes*)*.

STEP FOUR: Assign students the following narratives: Nadia el-Kareem (13 pp.), and John Mayik (22 pp). Students should begin reading the narratives on their own or in small groups. Encourage them to employ active reading strategies. During their reading, students should post questions and responses on the KWL chart, as well as look for quotes that reflect the narrator's viewpoints on *home, family, exile* and the label *refugee*. (15 minutes).

The remainder of the reading should be done as homework and/or during the beginning of the next class period.

STEP FIVE: Introduce storyboards as a tool to help visually express and summarize reading. If students are unfamiliar with storyboards, provide examples (there are many appropriate examples online). Give students a copy of the Storyboards handout, which includes definitions and a sample storyboard format. Each student or small group can choose the narrative they would like to make a storyboard from, or each student or group can do a storyboard for both (5–7 minutes).

DAY TWO

STEP ONE: If needed, allow time for students to finish their reading (10 minutes).

STEP TWO: As a warm-up activity, students should post any responses/questions from their reading on the KWL chart (5 minutes).

STEP THREE: Working alone or in small groups, students begin work on their storyboards. Pens, pencils, magazines (to cut images out of), tape and other classroom supplies should be readily accessible. Allow students to share ideas and discuss text evidence that communicates their narrator's viewpoints regarding *home*, *family*, *exile*, and the label *refugee*. Remind students that they are practicing their summarizing and storytelling skills and that art or drawing expertise is not necessary to create a successful storyboard. If students need more time to complete their storyboards, take time at the beginning of the next class period. If students are working individually, storyboards can be completed as homework (35–40 minutes).

DAY THREE

STEP ONE: If needed, allow time for students to finish their storyboards (10 minutes).

STEP TWO: Have groups (or individuals) tape their storyboards around the classroom in museum or art gallery-style. Narrators should have their own "section" of the gallery (5 minutes).

STEP THREE: Students do a "gallery walk" of the classroom, silently examining the storyboards. During the walk, students may post questions and responses on the KWL chart (10 minutes).

STEP FOUR: Utilizing responses from the KWL chart, class has a discussion related to the storyboards and how they reflect the challenges and complexities of the labels "exile" and "refugee" (10–15 minutes).

DISCUSSION QUESTIONS:

- *How do the storyboards allow you to personalize the experience of the narrators?*
- *How did this activity help you to understand the labels "exile" and "refugee?"*
- *Can you think of the power that labels have in your own life? What are they?*
- *What are some of the ways in which* home *and* family *are represented in the Storyboards?*
- *Are there "internal" exiles or refugees within the United States? Who are they? Can you think of any examples from U.S. history?*

STEP FIVE: Conclude the unit by allowing students to fill in the "L" section of the KWL chart. They should also feel free to add to the "K" and "W" sections (5–7 minutes).

STORYBOARDS

DEFINITION OF A STORYBOARD: A consecutive set of panels on which images and words are arranged to show the important changes of action and emotion in a series of "shots" (as for a film, television show, music video, comic, graphic novel, etc.).

STORYBOARD DIRECTIONS: On your storyboard, create a nonverbal representation of the text evidence of Nadia's or John's viewpoints, experiences or attitudes regarding *home*, *family*, *exile*, and the label *refugee.* You can make your storyboard larger if you would like. Create your panels as a story with a beginning, middle, and end, mirroring the chronology of your assigned narrative. Fill the blocks of the storyboard with stick figures, magazine cutouts, drawings, etc. Include text "bubbles" for the actual verbal text evidence. Then, below the storyboard, state the narrator's viewpoint or attitude as reflected in the passage.

STEP SIX (optional): Essay or Journal Writing.

The storyboard lesson and accompanying KWL chart should yield many topics worthy of further exploration and reflection. Class can consider several topics for a personal essay or journal entry related to the unit (can be done during class or assigned as homework). Class may also want to read other narratives from *Out of Exile* (as suggested in **Connections**).

POSSIBLE TOPICS INCLUDE:

- *How do you define* home*? How many definitions directly apply to your life?*
- *Do the terms* refugee *or* exile *resonate with you personally? If so, how?*
- *If you were exiled from your home or family, what would you miss the most?*
- *Can you compare/contrast the narrator's experience with an individual or group you consider to be "internal" refugees within the United States?*

POSSIBLE ORAL HISTORY PROJECT: Class creates an oral history project focusing on definitions and realities of *home* and *family*. Project can examine the myriad ways in which individuals construct their own versions of both.

MEDIA OPTION: Documentary films:

Lost Boys of Sudan (dirs. Megan Mylan and Jon Shenk). POV/P.B.S., 2004. *Lost Boys of Sudan* is an Emmy-nominated feature-length documentary that follows two Sudanese refugees on an extraordinary journey from Africa to America.

Museum of Exile: Assyrian Youth in Chicago (dir. Wonjung Bae). a twelve-minute HD documentary film that tells the story of teenage refugees from Iraq who go to Niles West High School in Skokie, Illinois. (*vimeo.com/14793548*)

EXPLORING DISPLACEMENT THROUGH THE FIVE SENSES

———————

TIME NEEDED: Two class periods.

MATERIALS: Emilia Gonzalez narrative from *Throwing Stones at the Moon* (p. 25–44), or excerpt (p. 32–35), four pieces of butcher paper with quotes from the text, markers, dry erase board/pens.

OBJECTIVE: Through analysis, discussion, and a written visual imagery exercise, students will be able to develop a deeper, empathic understanding of the text and the realities of being a displaced person. Students will hone literacy skills through reading and analyzing text and writing original poems.

RELATED CORE CURRICULUM STANDARDS: Speaking and Listening SL.9–10.1, SL.9–10.5. Writing W.9–10.3. Language L.9–10.5. Reading History RH.9–10.2, RH.9–10.4

CONNECTIONS: Lessons can also be used with any narratives from *Throwing Stones at the Moon* in addition to any narratives from *Out of Exile*. Other Voice of Witness narratives that can be used for this lesson: Zenzele, Amos, Violet, Boniface, John, and Alice from *Hope Deferred*; and Tan Htay, Saw Moe, and Khine Su from *Nowhere To Be Home*.

NARRATIVE EXCERPT: "We spent the whole night with the doors open, as the paras had told us to. We talked about what had happened, tried to account for other villagers and count the dead but we spoke quietly since the paras were passing by all the houses. The paramilitaries came by the houses and threw live chickens at us and said, 'Here, eat this, it's yours.' *We asked ourselves, What will become of us? Where will we go?"* —Emilia Gonzalez

OVERVIEW

This lesson encourages students to develop deeper empathy with the narrators in *Throwing Stones at the Moon* by recalling a time in which they, themselves, felt isolated, displaced, or disempowered. Students will read and analyze the narrative through a lens of visual imagery while honing their literary skills through a poetry exercise. By crafting precise, detailed images, students will connect more personally to the issues they are writing and reading about.

DAY ONE

STEP ONE: As a warm up activity, students respond to the following written prompt (5 minutes):

* *When you see police, military, or government officials, how do you feel—safe, protected, threatened, something else? Explain.*

STEP TWO: Pair Share: Assign each student a partner, with whom they will share and discuss their responses to the prompt (5 minutes).

STEP THREE: Using popcorn reading* or another reading strategy that meets the needs of your class, read Emilia Gonzalez's narrative aloud. Ask students to highlight/underline exceptional imagery as they are listening to the text. At the end of the excerpt, check for understanding, and ask students if the passages they highlighted emphasized the emotion of the narrative (40 minutes).

STEP FOUR: On the board, give a brief lesson on imagery in writing (see following handout) (10 minutes).

STEP FIVE: As a closing discussion, ask the students how Emilia's narrative was strengthened through the use of visual imagery (10 minutes).

DAY TWO

STEP ONE: Have a piece of butcher paper on each of the four walls, each with a short excerpt from Emilia's narrative that is rich with imagery. Suggestions:

- *Later, the villagers learned that the paramilitaries had killed five people in the park. They'd killed a teacher who was still in her nightgown, a man and his son, and another boy.*
- *During the three nights I stayed there with Alberto, we made a fire at the door for light, and to fight off the mosquitoes. I couldn't sleep. I heard things. I thought I heard gunshots.*
- *One of them grabbed {the girl's} long hair and wrapped it around his hand, like you wrap a towel, and they dragged her away. They took her to an orange tree away from the court and killed her.*
- *The first to be killed was a friend of Carlos's, who was sitting next to him. The paras grabbed him and lopped off his ear, and then they put a black bag over his head and started stabbing him and asking questions. When he died, he fell into my son's lap.*

Divide students into groups of four, and have them walk around the room and respond to each piece of imagery on the butcher paper. Give them the following prompts (15 minutes):

- *How does this make you feel?*
- *What comes up for you when you read this excerpt?*
- *Which type of imagery is exemplified here?*
- *Does the imagery make you feel more connected to the narrator and/or the story?*

STEP TWO: After each group has visited all four pieces of butcher paper, ask students to return to their seats. Have each student write a short poem—composed solely of lines of imagery—about a time in their life when they felt threatened, displaced, or unprotected. If they are stuck, suggest that they write a poem of five stanzas (*a group of lines within a poem, set off from other groups of lines by a space*), each stanza drawing on one of the five senses (I saw _____, I heard _____, I felt _____, I smelled _____, I tasted _____) (*30 minutes*).

---

* To use popcorn reading, call on a student to begin reading aloud, and ask her to read as long as she wants to. When she's ready to pass the reading onto someone else, she'll say "popcorn" followed by another student's name.

USING IMAGERY IN POETRY WRITING

Imagery can be defined as the use of descriptive language to form mental images in writing. Imagery makes writing memorable and unique. Think about the five senses—seeing, hearing, tasting, touching, and smelling—and how you can use them to incorporate imagery into your writing.

Be as specific as you can! Below is an example of a five senses chart using the following prompt:

Describe being at a state fair on a summer evening.

SEEING	HEARING	TASTING	TOUCHING	SMELLING
the ferris wheel is a kaleidoscope of color	*the ride operator's voice sounds like car wheels driving over gravel*	*my funnel cake is thick with warmth as I bite through its sugary crust*	*I sit on a worn, sun-faded bench, tracing a hole in the wood with my finger*	*the night air smells bitter and sweet, like pennies and sugar*

Using the following prompt, fill out your own five senses chart:

Describe being lost in the aisles of an old library.

SEEING	HEARING	TASTING	TOUCHING	SMELLING

STEP THREE: Ask for volunteers to share their poems with the class (10 minutes).

STEP FOUR: After students have shared their poems, facilitate a closing discussion based on the following prompts: (10 minutes)

- *Did your poems connect to the theme of displacement in Emilia's narrative?*
- *Do you feel that your home, and/or your ideas about home, contribute to your sense of identity?*
- *How does strong, visual imagery strengthen the message of the poems?*
- *Do you feel more empathy for the narrator when you are presented with imagery that enables you to see* (hear, taste, smell, touch) *what she is going through? Describe.*

STEP FIVE (OPTIONAL): As homework, challenge students to collect five examples of word-images (*descriptive things people say, word-images they find in books or magazines, etc.*) related to themes of displacement, and bring them in to share with the class the following day.

POSSIBLE ORAL HISTORY PROJECT: Class creates an oral history project focusing on definitions and realities of *home* and *family*. Project can examine the myriad ways in which individuals construct their own versions of both.

1. Students identify refugees, immigrants, and/or anyone who has faced civil war or government corruption (possible guest speaker opportunity). Working in groups, students brainstorm a list of initial questions for the narrator, and work toward a group interview/oral history narrative.
2. Students identify a family member or friend to interview about a time in their life when they felt isolated, displaced, or disempowered. Teacher leads students through a full oral history project: interview, transcription, narrative editing, and final presentation.

MEDIA OPTION: Organizational Website: Forced Migration Online (FMO). Forced Migration Online provides online access to a diverse range of resources concerning the situation of forced migrants worldwide. The website is coordinated by a team based at the Refugee Studies Centre, Department of International Development, University of Oxford. (*www.forcedmigration.org*)

ASSIGNING LABELS

TIME NEEDED: Two class periods.

MATERIALS: *Refugee Hotel* (with selected images), sticky notes (2 colors), red markers, pencils, whiteboard.

OBJECTIVE: To develop self-awareness and critical thinking skills by exploring assumptions and the power of labels, using written and visual narratives from *Refugee Hotel*.

RELATED CORE CURRICULUM STANDARDS: Reading History RH.9–10.1, RH.11–12.1, RH.9–10.2, RH.1--12.2, RH.11–12.7 Speaking and Listening SL.9–10.1, SL.11–12.1, SL.9–10.2, SL.11–12.2

CONNECTIONS: This activity can be adapted for any narrative from the Voice of Witness series with a set of related photographs or images.

ESSENTIAL QUESTIONS:

- *How do we label others?*
- *What assumptions do we bring with us when interacting with new people—especially those who are different from us?*

NARRATIVE EXCERPT: "To be called a refugee is bad. It means I have no country, no home, and that I'll always be running away . . . That's why I came to the United States, in 2009, with my husband and children. This is a good country for refugees; once I become an American I can get everything an American has, and I will never be called a refugee again." —*Orenie Ndayishimiye*

TEACHER PREPARATION: Take some time to become familiar with the recent history of Burma (Myanmar). Among other sources, the *New York Times* Country Profile of Myanmar is a good place to start (especially as it is constantly updated). *Human Rights Watch: World Report Burma* is another good (and updated) resource. This information should be compiled into a one-page Burma Fact Sheet for students.

DAY ONE

STEP ONE: As a warm-up activity, ask students to write silently in their journals, reflecting on the following prompts (5 minutes):

- *What is an assumption?*
- *What are ways that we make assumptions about other people?*
- *Why do we do this?*

STEP TWO: Have a class conversation based on the warm-up activity, inviting students to "share out" from their journal reflections (5–7 minutes).

STEP THREE: Introduce labels by facilitating a short class discussion using the following suggested prompt (5–7 minutes):

When we encounter someone who seems different from us—different country, age, ethnicity, and personality— we automatically try to understand them, so we fill in the blanks about who they are. This is natural— but do we sometimes make assumptions that are wrong or unfair?

STEP FOUR: Have students do a "pair-share" in which they discuss the following with a classmate (5–7 minutes):

Talk about a time when you have been LABELED—when someone made an assumption about you. What happened? What was that like? What was your response?

Now talk about a time when you've labeled someone else, and have maybe felt badly about the label you put on him or her. What was that like? Did you learn anything from that?

STEP FIVE: Have a short class discussion allowing students to share out from their pair-share conversations. During the share out, encourage students to explore and investigate how and why we label things, in order for them to transform and expand their understanding of people different from themselves.

The following suggested prompts can be used during the discussion (10 minutes):

- *Where do our labels come from?*
- *Why do we label things?*
- *Is this a natural or unnatural thing? How can it be positive—and how can it be negative?*

STEP SIX: Briefly introduce *Refugee Hotel* using information from the introduction and other sources, if desired. Create a frame of reference for the book that centers on refugees being a group that has been both socially and legally "labeled." On the whiteboard, write the following quotes and definitions (5 minutes):

- *"To be called a refugee is bad. It means I have no country, no home, and that I'll always be running away." Orenie Ndayishimiye from* Refugee Hotel
- *Definition of a refugee: "A refugee is a person who has fled persecution based on his/her race, religion, political opinion, nationality, or membership in a particular social group."*

STEP SEVEN: In small groups, students reflect together on the differences and similarities between the legal definition of a refugee, and Ndayishimiye's experience of being labeled as a refugee. (7 minutes) Suggested guiding questions:

- *What is persecution? What might some examples be?*
- *What is the connection between being persecuted and being "labeled"?*
- *What does Orenie Ndayishimiye mean when she says "to be called a refugee is bad"?*
- *What are labels we often assign to refugees?*

STEP EIGHT: Have a short class discussion allowing students to share out from their small group conversations. Possible discussion prompt (10 minutes):

Refugees have essentially been "labeled" as different, and persecuted because of that label. And then they have been re-labeled as refugees. What else came up in your conversations?

DAY TWO

STEP ONE: Hang a dozen or so photographs from *Refugee Hotel* (from both parts of the book) around the room. Class then does a "gallery walk," examining and exploring the photographs. If needed, remind students that these are images of refugees who have come to rebuild their lives in the U.S. (5–7 minutes). As students engage with the photographs, encourage them to consider the following:

- *Who are these people?*
- *Where do they come from?*
- *What are they experiencing?*
- *What are their emotions?*
- *What is their background?*

STEP TWO: Each student is then given 3 or so sticky notes that will serve as "labels." They will then attach a one-word label to a photograph of their choice. Remind students that the activity requires courage and honesty. Sharing examples such as "sad," "confused," "missing," "alone," etc., may be useful in getting the activity started (5–7 minutes).

After students have placed all of their labels, the class does another gallery walk, reexamining the images and the labels that have been assigned to them (5 minutes).

STEP THREE: In groups of 3–5, students are assigned to read aloud different narratives from *Refugee Hotel* (10–15 minutes). Suggested narratives: Do Lian Zam (aka Elis); Tsehai Wodajo; Heinay Moo; Orenie Ndayishimiye; Susil Ghalley.

After reading, groups discuss their stories using the following suggested prompts (7–10 minutes):

- *What are the ways in which the narrator has been labeled?*
- *What labels did you assign to the narrator at the beginning, when you first started reading? Did these change by the end?*
- *What labels did the narrator assign to others in the story?*
- *What labels does the narrator put on his/her home—on America?*

STEP FOUR: Re-labeling: After reading and discussing the narrator's stories, students may feel that their initial labels might be deepened or rounded by knowing more of their background. Using different color sticky notes, encourage students to add additional "labels" to the photographs (10 minutes). Before starting the activity, provide the following instruction:

- *What is missing from the previous labels?*
- *If a previous label seems truer now, use the marker to make a red star.*
- *If a label seems wrong, put an X on it (not over the writing).*
- *Not all original labels will become irrelevant or wrong, but knowing more of the narrator's story might deepen the initial label.*

STEP FIVE: Class does another gallery walk, silently reexamining the images and additional labels (5 minutes).

STEP SIX: As a class, discuss the Assigning Labels lesson using the following suggested prompts (10 minutes):

- *Did reading the stories change our opinions and assumptions about the photographs? If so, how?*
- *Did the stories make us more or less compassionate towards the people in the photographs?*
- *What does knowing details about someone change about our understanding of them?*

STEP SEVEN: Written Reflection (can be done as homework assignment): Students reflect on the lesson by responding to the following prompt (15+ minutes):

How can we be mindful about the labels we assign ourselves and each other?

POSSIBLE ORAL HISTORY/PHOTO ESSAY PROJECT: Students conduct oral history interviews with friends, family, and members of their school community, creating interview questions that reflect the essential questions of the labeling lesson. Students can build on themes from their pair shares, group discussions, readings and written reflections. The project could also include a photo essay that visually represents these themes.

LESSON 12

IMEGES AND EXAMINATIONS OF *HOME*

_____

TIME NEEDED: Two class periods.

MATERIALS: *Refugee Hotel*, journals, cameras.

OBJECTIVE: To explore personal and political definitions of home, family, and resettlement through an analysis of, and creative response to, the photographs and written narratives in *Refugee Hotel*.

RELATED CORE CURRICULUM STANDARDS: Speaking and Listening SL.9–10.1, SL.11–12.1, SL.9–10.2, SL.11–12.2, SL.9–10.4, SL.11–12.4 Writing W.9–10.2, W.11–12.2

CONNECTIONS: This activity can be adapted for narratives from *Out of Exile*, *Underground America*, *Hope Deferred*, and *Nowhere to Be Home* with a set of related photographs or images.

ESSENTIAL QUESTIONS:

- *How do we define "home"? Is it where we were born, where we spent most of our lives, the country of our origin?*
- *Why is it that certain objects—artifacts, heirlooms, memorabilia—are irreplaceable, and carry with them such strong feelings of home?*
- *How is home defined in a political or institutional context?*

NARRATIVE EXCERPT: "Because we'd lost everything, it didn't matter where we went, so we decided to keep moving. Our family signed up, and it took one year to be called. Then we came to Fargo." —*Rup Khatiwada*

"It's hard to balance my American experience—working, living like an American—and my Nepali and Bhutanese traditions."—*Prem Khatiwada*

DAY ONE

STEP ONE: As a warm-up activity, ask students to write silently in their journals, reflecting on the following prompt (5 minutes):

- *If you were forced to leave your country of origin and could only carry a small suitcase, what would you carry with you and why? What would you deem as necessary? What would be crucial reminders of home?*

STEP TWO: Have a "pair share" conversation based on the warm-up activity, encouraging students to share out from their journal reflections (5–7 minutes).

STEP THREE: Briefly Introduce *Refugee Hotel* using information/context from the introduction and/ or A Brief Guide to Resettlement from the back of the book. Suggested information includes: Introduction: Please Pardon Our Dust, What is a Refugee (p. 290), Refugee Status (p. 290–291), The Resettlement Process (p. 291), and Assurance and Arrival (p. 293). After reading this background information, have a group discussion using the following suggested prompts (15 minutes):

- *Using the Brief Guide to Resettlement as a jumping off point, how does the idea of home change during the act of resettlement?*
- *Where do "home" and "resettlement" connect, converge, or diverge?*
- *In the Assurance and Arrival section, there is a "laundry list of necessities." Did some of the items on the list surprise you? What do you think should be included or excluded?*

STEP FOUR: What Do I See? (adapted from Project Zero)
Refugee Hotel has two large photographic sections. Have students look through the first set of photos in the book. Just looking—no talking or writing. Encourage students not to rush through the section too quickly (10–12 minutes).

STEP FIVE: Have students go through the first section again and write down what they notice in the pictures—what they actually *see* (roads, beds, windows, illuminated signs, etc). Encourage them to look for various themes or motifs (the American Dream, family, isolation, hope, etc.). Creating a "T Chart" with what students see on one side and themes/motifs on the other will help students distinguish between the two (15 minutes).

STEP SIX: Have a brief class discussion related to their observations, using the following suggested prompts (7–10 minutes):

- *What did you observe in these photographs?*
- *Were there recurring themes in the photographs? If so, what were they?*
- *How do these themes communicate the refugees' resettlement experience?*

STEP SEVEN: For homework, have students read Rup and Prem Khatiwada's narrative from *Refugee Hotel*. Encourage them to use active reading strategies (15–20 minutes).

DAY TWO

STEP ONE: As a warm up activity, have students do a pair share discussion using the following suggested prompt (5 minutes):

- *Describe a time in your life when you felt disoriented, out of place, or needed to adjust to new surroundings. You can describe this experience from a variety of perspectives—emotional, physical, environmental, or spiritual, just to name a few.*

STEP TWO: Have a class conversation based on the warm-up activity, inviting students to share out from their pair share conversations. Encourage students to reference the Assurance and Arrival section of *Refugee Hotel* and Rup and Prem Khatiwada's narrative (10 minutes).

STEP THREE (PHOTO ESSAY PROJECT): Incorporating information from the prior share out, inform students that they will be assigned to select and photograph 8–10 items in their homes that they believe to be absolutely necessary in creating their own "laundry list of necessities" for resettlement (10 minutes). Any kind of camera is acceptable (disposable, digital, phone, computer, etc). Encourage students to consider how their choices will reflect the following themes:

- *Transition*
- *Resettlement*
- *Family culture/traditions*
- *Home*

The following narrator quotes from *Refugee Hotel* can inspire and help frame student work on the assignment:

"To me, home is a place where you can stay forever: you don't have to leave or move around." —*Farah Ibrahim*, p. 113

"I feel safe here. I can think about my future and my family's future—I can plan for tomorrow, next week, next month. In Iraq, all we cared about was surviving one more day." —*Farah Ibrahim*, p. 116

"For me, it's difficult because I have family in Iraq, so it will always be my home. But at the same time home is where you feel safe, and where you find all that you love: family and friends." —*Mahmmoud Dawoodi*, p. 117

"My parents were born in Burma, and I was born in Thailand, but I'm not sure I belong anywhere. I can't go back and live in Thailand now that I've come to America. I live here in Charlottesville, but I have no real home; lots of Karen people are leaving this place. But for now this is my destiny, it's what has happened to me. And you never know what will happen to you." —*Heinay Moo*, p. 120

STEP FOUR: Once the assignment has been completed (time to complete the assignment will vary), students will present a brief slide show of their selected photographs. After all students have presented, have a class discussion using the following suggested prompts (15–20 minutes):

- *How did the photographs and narratives from* Refugee Hotel *inspire your photo essay? Can you cite specific examples?*
- *What differences and similarities did you see in comparison to the Refugee Service checklist?*
- *What similarities arose, and what differences appeared within the photo essays?*
- *How were the themes of the assignment (transition, home, etc.) expressed in the photo essays? Please cite several examples.*

STEP FIVE: Written Reflection (can be done as homework assignment): Students reflect on the lesson by responding to one of the narrator quotes used to frame the photo essay project (15+ minutes). Encourage them to make personal connections to the narrators and reference photographs from the book as well as their own, in addition to reflecting on themes and definitions of home, resettlement, and the challenges that arise from adjusting to new environments while maintaining ties to family culture and traditions.

POSSIBLE ORAL HISTORY/PHOTO ESSAY PROJECT: Students in the class can conduct oral history interviews with friends, family, or community members who have recently resettled to the U.S. Interview questions can be based on themes, motifs, and ideas from the lesson. Students can also interview each other and share personal stories based on the images they photographed for the photo essay assignment.

U.S. JUSTICE

OVERVIEW

This unit explores the flawed and complicated nature of the U.S. criminal justice system through the stories of wrongfully convicted and exonerated individuals. It enables students to experience this system as an extension of a society they have a personal stake in, rather than as a disembodied, faceless bureaucracy. In the process, students can empathize with the plight of each narrator, personalizing the details of how these human beings were stripped of their identity.

SURVIVING JUSTICE

––––––––––––

TIME NEEDED: Three to four class periods (five-day lesson plan available on website).

MATERIALS: *Surviving Justice: America's Wrongly Convicted and Exonerated* narratives: Juan Melendez (30 pp.), Gary Gauger (30 pp.), Joseph Amrine (36 pp.), Scenario for Surviving Justice, Exoneree Worksheet, Stand Up/Sit Down Exercise, and Talk to the Text handout.

OBJECTIVE: Making personal connections to wrongful incarceration, the death penalty, and other aspects of the U.S. criminal justice system

RELATED CORE CURRICULUM STANDARDS: Reading History RH.9–10.2, RH.9–10.4, RH.9–10.10. Speaking and Listening SL.9–10.1, SL.11–12.1, SL.9–10.2, SL.11–12.2.

NARRATIVE EXCERPT: "When the trial first got started, I was like, 'I can't believe this. This has gone on long enough now.' The second day of the trial, my lawyer told me, he leans over and says, 'We're halfway home.' I'm looking at him saying, 'Halfway to death row,' because what I'd seen of the trial so far, it didn't look good for me. Because they had two guys who claimed they'd seen the murder, and I'd committed the murder. They had Terry Russell, who claimed I told him I committed the murder. The main thing I was thinking was, 'How are they going to believe inmates over the guard?' And that's one point I could never get past, that they actually took the inmates' word over the guard. So that was going through my mind. The guard was in the room when it happened. And the guard identified another guy as the one who committed the murder." —*Joseph Amrine*

DAY ONE

STEP ONE: Before reading any of the narratives, students should participate in the warm-up activity on the next page (10 minutes).

SURVIVING JUSTICE

———————

Read the following scenario and *completely* answer the questions that follow.

One Saturday afternoon, you are arrested while you are walking down the block to a friend's house. You are charged with aggravated assault and robbery.

While the police are questioning you, you find out that, at 4 a.m. the previous evening, a man stopped his car at a stop sign just one block away from your house and was pulled from his car. He was brutally beaten and had fifty dollars in cash stolen from his wallet. He claims that his assailant was wearing a mask, but your body and style of dress match his description exactly (it also matches most of the people in your neighborhood). Coincidentally, the police find *exactly* fifty dollars in *your* wallet.

You repeatedly tell the police that you are innocent and that you spent the previous evening sleeping, that you went to bed at 10 p.m. and woke up at 8 a.m. Since you were sleeping alone and your parents were out of town, there is *no one* to prove you were home the entire time, and you cannot provide an alibi for the time of the crime.

During your trial, the attorney assigned to you instructs you to remain silent, and when you attempt to speak to defend yourself (since the attorney is not doing it), the judge silences you and threatens to remove you from the courtroom entirely if you do not remain quiet.

You listen as the prosecution presents its case, and even you have to admit that it sounds like you *could* have committed this crime. Despite the fact that there is not very much evidence against you, the jury (which is made up of twelve people of a different race from you) very quickly deliberates and finds you guilty as charged. You have *never* admitted to the crime and have continued to vigorously insist that you are innocent. Because of your earlier outbursts, you are not allowed to speak after your sentence is handed down: ten years in prison.

1. Given these circumstances, is there anything you could have done to prevent your incarceration?

2. How would you convince others of your innocence once you were in prison?

STEP TWO: Students do a "pair share" by sharing their answers with a neighbor (5–7 minutes).

STEP THREE: Ask pairs to share their ideas, and discuss them as a class (15 minutes). Possible discussion prompts:

- *How did your opinions about your community influence your answers?*
- *Did your beliefs about our justice system influence your answers?*
- *Did any direct or indirect experiences shape your answers?*

STEP FOUR: Introduce *Surviving Justice* and read pages 3–7 of the introduction as a class (10–15 minutes). Take time to answer any questions. Refer to the glossary of *Surviving Justice* for vocabulary terms.

STEP FIVE: Ask pairs to share their ideas, and discuss them as a class (15 minutes). Possible discussion prompts:

- *How did your opinions about your community influence your answers?*
- *Did your beliefs about our justice system influence your answers?*
- *Did any direct or indirect experiences shape your answers?*

STEP SIX: Assign one of the following narratives to each student as homework: Juan Melendez (26 pp.), Gary Gauger (26 pp.), or Joseph Amrine (31 pp.). Please add additional time for reading (either as homework or during class) if needed. Students should use active reading strategies such as the Talk to the Text handout on page 23 to generate questions for group discussion.

DAY TWO

STEP ONE: If needed, begin with additional time for reading and reflection (time will vary).

STEP TWO: Working in groups according to their assigned narratives, students discuss comments from their Talk to the Text worksheets. Assign a facilitator and note-taker for each group. The facilitator will be responsible for asking the group to share comments, opinions, potential answers, and making sure to get feedback from each member of the group. The note-taker is responsible for writing down the key points of the discussion. Each student should share at least five comments— one of each type from the worksheet (20 minutes).

STEP THREE: Using the notes from their group discussion, facilitators report the key ideas and comments to the entire class, encouraging students from other groups to comment on and answer one another's questions (10 minutes).

STEP FOUR: During class or as homework, students complete the attached *Surviving Justice* Exoneree Worksheet (20–25 minutes).

SURVIVING JUSTICE
EXONEREE WORKSHEET

NAME OF EXONEREE:
CRIME EXONEREE WAS CONVICTED OF:
HOW LONG WAS THIS PERSON IMPRISONED?:

1. Give some background about the person you studied, e.g., where they are from, what their family or personal life was like. Be sure to mention details pertinent to the case.

2. Describe the crime of which this person was accused.

3. How did this person come to be linked to the crime?

4. How does the exoneree describe his or her experiences in prison? How did maintaining his or her innocence affect his or her time in prison? Did it make it more or less difficult?

5. What was life like for this person after he or she was released from prison? How did the label of "exoneree" affect him or her?

STEP ONE: Have students write a one-paragraph response to the following prompt (5–7 minutes):

- *Do you think it is possible that you could be arrested for a crime you did not commit? Why or why not?*

STEP TWO: Ask the class to share their responses to the prompt. Make sure to refer back to the exoneree's narratives for counterexamples (5–7 minutes).

STEP THREE: Conduct the Stand Up/Sit Down Exercise. Instructions are below (5 minutes).

STAND UP/SIT DOWN INSTRUCTIONS
(adapted from Bay Area Police Watch, an organization that assists survivors of police misconduct and brutality).

EXPLANATION OF THE ACTIVITY: The facilitator will read out a statement and if the statement is true for you, then you stand up. If the statement is not true for you, stay seated.

STATEMENTS:

- o **Stand up** if you have been harassed or stopped by the police.

- o **Stand up** if you have been harassed in or followed around a store.

- o **Stand up** if you feel like the laws in this country are set up to protect you.

- o **Stand up** if you or someone you know has been falsely accused of a crime.

- o **Stand up** if you feel the police will protect you if you need to call on them.

- o **Stand up** if you feel the police only use force when necessary.

- o **Stand up** if you or someone you know has been a victim of police misconduct.

- o **Stand up** if you have ever felt intimidated by the police.

- o **Stand up** if you feel the police have the right to stop and search you with no warrant.

- o **Stand up** if you feel community members should work in conjunction with the police when it comes to policing their community.

STEP FOUR: After the statements have been read out, break up the group into pairs to process out any thoughts or feelings the exercise brought up. They can either choose to share a story that related to one of the statements or else share general reflections (5 minutes).

STEP FIVE: Invite anyone to share with the entire group. During your discussion, consider the following questions (15 minutes):

- *Were you surprised by who stood and sat? Why?*
- *How did it feel to stand/sit?*
- *What does this exercise tell you?*
- *How does our community handle these issues?*
- *As a society, what contributes to this "cycle" of conduct or behavior?*

STEP SIX: Conclude the unit by referring back to the narratives from *Surviving Justice.* Ask students to share their responses to the following questions (5–7 minutes):

- *What in your* Surviving Justice *narrative surprised you?*
- *What is most important to you in the narrative you read?*

STEP SEVEN: (optional): Have students respond to the following essay prompt:

"Men simply copied the realities of their hearts when they built prisons."

—Richard Wright

In a well-developed essay, explain how the experiences of one of the narrators from *Surviving Justice* support or refute this statement.

POSSIBLE ORAL HISTORY PROJECT: Class creates an oral history project focusing on wrongful conviction and incarceration of youth, examining juvenile justice and youth violence in their community.

MEDIA OPTION: Organizational Websites:
American Civil Liberties Union Download: *What to Do If You're Stopped By Police, Immigration Agents or the FBI: www.aclu.org/drug-law-reform-immigrants-rights-racial-justice/know-your-rights-what-do-if-you*
Center on Wrongful Convictions of Youth: *www.cwcy.org*
The Innocence Project: *www.innocenceproject.org*
Life After Exoneration Program: *www.exonerated.org/content*

SECURITY

"It stands as a caution that, in times of international hostility and antagonisms, our institutions, legislative, executive and judicial, must be prepared to exercise their authority to protect all citizens from the petty fears and prejudices that are so easily aroused."

—Judge Marilyn Hall Patel
(*Korematsu v. U.S.*)

OVERVIEW

The balancing act between civil rights and security in the United States has always brought up complicated questions: is it necessary to suspend or ignore our civil rights in times of crisis or upheaval in order to maintain security? Or do these suspensions of rights make us less safe? There are many examples from U.S. history to draw from: President Roosevelt's executive order sending Japanese Americans to concentration camps throughout the country, and more recently, in the aftermath of 9/11, the controversies surrounding enemy combatants, the War on Terror, and aspects of the USA Patriot Act.

The narratives in *Patriot Acts: Narratives of Post-9/11 Injustice* bring home the realities of individuals who have found themselves subject to a wide range of civil rights abuses, allowing students to grapple with the human costs that lie at the heart of this pertinent contemporary issue.

CIVIL RIGHTS AND SECURITY

————————

TIME NEEDED: One class period.

MATERIALS: Narrative of Adama Bah from *Patriot Acts*, and a list of civil rights.

OBJECTIVE: To analyze U.S. civil rights and security issues through the lens of personal narrative.

RELATED CORE CURRICULUM STANDARDS: Reading History RH.9–10.3, RH.9–10.4, RH.9–10.9.

CONNECTIONS: This activity can also be done with the following narratives from *Patriot Acts*: Yassir Alladin Afifi, Faheem Muhammad, Raed Jarrar. The following narratives from the series can also be used: Patricia Thompson and Dan Bright from *Voices from the Storm*; Farid and Olga from *Underground America*.

NARRATIVE EXCERPT: "The morning of March 24, 2005, my family and I were in the house sleeping.

Someone knocked on the door, and my mom went and opened it. These men barged in, waking us up. I always sleep with the blanket over my head. They pull the blanket off my head, I look up, I see a man. He said, 'You've got to get out!' I'm like, *what the hell, what's going on?*

I saw about ten to fifteen people in our apartment and right outside our door in the hallway. They were mostly men, but there were two women. Some had FBI jackets, and others were from the police department and the DHS. We were all forced out of the bed and told to sit in the living room. They were going through papers, throwing stuff around, yelling and talking to each other, then whispering. I heard them yelling at my mother in the background, and my mom can't speak much English, and they were pulling her into the kitchen, yelling at her, 'We're going to deport you and your whole family!' —*Adama Bah*

STEP ONE: Examine and discuss the list of civil rights and address any questions. You may find it helpful to refer to specific examples of these rights (10–12 minutes).

Basic civil rights in the United States:

- Your **First Amendment rights**—freedom of speech, association, and assembly; freedom of the press, and freedom of religion.
- Your right to **equal protection under the law**—protection against unlawful discrimination.
- Your right to **due process**—fair treatment by the government whenever the loss of your liberty or property is at stake.
- Your right to **privacy**—freedom from unwarranted government intrusion into your personal and private affairs.

STEP TWO: Read pp. 29–41 of Adama Bah's narrative. Reading can be done as a class or in small groups. Encourage students to practice active reading strategies.

STEP THREE: Compare the list of civil rights with the Adama Bah narrative. Discuss the following questions (20 minutes):

- *Were the civil rights of Adama Bah violated? If so, which ones?*
- *If these rights were violated, was it justified for the sake of security?*
- *Adama Bah's experience was related to the passage of the USA Patriot Act in 2001. Can you think of other related examples from U.S. history?*
- *In times of upheaval or crisis, is it necessary to suspend some of our civil rights in order to maintain security? Why or why not?*

ADDITIONAL DISCUSSION QUESTION:

- *What is your opinion of heightened airport security (body scans, searches, etc.)? Is it a necessary precaution or a violation of an individual's right to privacy?*

POSSIBLE ORAL HISTORY PROJECT: Class creates an oral history project that focuses on security and civil rights issues. Students conduct interviews with friends, family, local leaders and community members, collecting a variety of stories that reflect this divisive issue. The discussion questions above can be used as a basis for potential interview questions.

MEDIA OPTION: StandUP! is the ACLU's website for students and young people. (*www.aclu.org/standup*)

Islamic Networks Group (ING) is a nonprofit organization whose mission is to counter prejudice and discrimination against American Muslims by teaching about their traditions and contributions in the context of America's history and cultural diversity, while building relations between American Muslims and other groups. (*www.ing.org*)

GRAFFITI WALL EXERCISE

TIME NEEDED: One to two class periods.

MATERIALS: *Patriot Acts: Narratives of Post-9/11 Injustice*, poster-size sticky notes or large pieces of butcher paper, tape, and large felt-tip markers.

OBJECTIVE: To encourage personal responses to contemporary issues through interpretation, analysis, and empathy.

RELATED CORE CURRICULUM STANDARDS: Reading History RH.9–10.2. RH.9–10.3, RH.9–10.4.

CONNECTIONS: This activity can be done with any narrative from the Voice of Witness series.

NARRATIVE EXCERPT: "Sometimes I saw other Sikh kids being picked on at school. I felt really bad because I wanted to help them, but usually I didn't do anything. I had to look after myself. Whenever I could help, the kids I helped would avoid me. They would tell me, "Just stay away." I think it's probably because they were going through problems too. All of us were going through it." —*Gurwinder Singh*

STEP ONE: Read Gurwinder Singh's narrative from *Patriot Acts* (11 pages) as a class or in small groups. Encourage students to practice active reading strategies (20 minutes).

STEP TWO:

1. Hang large pieces of butcher paper or poster-size sticky notes on the wall.
2. Using individual words, quotations, questions, drawings, and symbols, have students post on the "Graffiti Wall" their feelings, responses, and questions related to the narratives. If it is a large class, you can split into two or more groups for this part of the activity (10 minutes).
3. Have the class silently "examine" the wall(s) (5–7 minutes).

    Facilitate a class discussion based on what the wall communicates about students' personal responses to the narrative.

DISCUSSION QUESTIONS (15–20 minutes):

- *Do any themes emerge (inequality, prejudice, etc.)? Any seeming contradictions?*
- *Does the wall somehow capture the narrator's experience? How?*
- *How does oral history help personalize the issues represented on the wall?*

POSSIBLE ORAL HISTORY PROJECT: Take the main themes from the Graffiti Wall and use them as the basis for oral history interviews within the class and school community.

WOMEN'S RIGHTS

OVERVIEW

Using narratives from *Inside This Place, Not of It: Narratives from Women's Prisons*, this unit delves into the lives of women in U.S. prisons. It explores gender bias, reproductive rights, and the ways in which race and class contribute to the harsh realities for women caught up in the U.S. criminal justice system.

INSIDE THIS PLACE, NOT OF IT: BODY STORIES

TIME NEEDED: Three class periods.

MATERIALS: *Inside This Place, Not of It*, large pieces of paper, and felt-tip markers.

OBJECTIVE: To analyze criminal justice issues through personal narratives.

RELATED CURRICULUM STANDARDS: Reading History RH.9–10.1, RH.9–10.5, RH.9–10.7. Speaking and Listening SL.9–10.1, SL.9–10.2.

CONNECTIONS: Body Stories and Letter Writing activities can be adapted for any narratives in the Voice of Witness series. Other narratives from *Inside This Place, Not of It* can be substituted for the ones listed below.

NARRATIVE EXCERPT: "I was there about a month before I actually saw a doctor. I didn't have vitamins there, and I had no prenatal care. I didn't really complain if I was in pain or anything, because the infirmary was real nasty. There was poo on the walls. It was just nasty. Then one day, when I was seven months pregnant, the guards called me down. They shackled my stomach and my feet and took me to see an OBGYN. I mean, you walk like this through the front door looking as if you've murdered someone, and I just thought it was really degrading. I know I made a mistake, but I don't think I deserved to be ashamed or embarrassed in this way. And even once I'd got in the back where the actual doctors' offices were, the shackles didn't come off. They took them off my feet, but nothing else; the shackles stayed on my stomach." —*Olivia Hamilton*

DAY ONE

STEP ONE: This warm-up activity focuses primarily on activating prior student knowledge of the issue. Have students create written responses to the following prompts (5 minutes):

- *What does it mean to be a criminal?*
- *What are prisons for?*

STEP TWO: Have students do a "pair-share" in which they discuss their responses to the prompts (5 minutes).

STEP THREE: Introduce *Inside This Place Not Of It*. Read and discuss predetermined sections of the Introduction (7–10 minutes).

STEP FOUR: Divide the class into groups of four to five students. Assign each group one of the following narratives from *Inside This Place, Not of It*: Francesca Salavieri (14 pp.), Olivia Hamilton

(14 pp.), Irma Rodriquez (12 pp.), Emily Madison (16 pp.), and Taisie Baldwin (12 pp.). Have each group read their assigned narrative. Groups can read aloud or silently. Encourage them to employ active reading strategies. Whatever they do not finish in class can be done as homework (30 minutes).

DAY TWO

STEP ONE: With large paper and markers, each group should draw a life-sized outline of a body. This is the body of their narrator. Using the following questions, encourage each group to fill it in according to how the narrator was affected by prison. Groups should also create five or six questions of their own (25 minutes):

BODY

How is _____ treated by doctors and nurses?

Does _____ receive the medication she needs?

Does _____ have all the knowledge she needs to best take care of herself?

How is _____'s body different after prison?

HEAD

What kind of privacy does _____ have?

How is _____ treated by guards and wardens? How does that affect her?

Does _____ receive any counseling or therapy?

HEART

Does _____ feel comfortable expressing her feelings in prison?

Does _____ have many friends in prison?

Does _____ receive visitors? What is the visiting process like?

If _____ has children, how has prison affected her relationships with them?

STEP TWO: Each group should present their "body story" to the rest of the class, explaining how they filled in their body and why. They should be able to refer to specific passages in the narrative as evidence for why they filled in the body as they did (*25 minutes*).

DAY THREE

STEP ONE: Have students write a letter to their narrator. Through their oral histories, the narrators have been talking to the students, telling them their stories. What do students want to say back? How do they want to respond? Remind them the narrators *spoke* their stories, so they should focus on writing an honest, heartfelt letter and not a formal essay (15 minutes).

STEP TWO: Returning to their narrative groups from the previous day, students read their letters aloud to one another, and reflect on the following questions (15 minutes):

- *How did you feel after reading the narrative? Do you think your letter conveys these feelings?*
- *Why did you choose to address the issues that you did?*
- *How would you hope your narrator would respond?*
- *If you were in your narrator's position, would you appreciate a letter like this?*
- *What else would you like to know about your narrator?*

STEP THREE: Have the class come together to generate the following two lists, incorporating the responses/findings from the previous activities (15 minutes):

- Major flaws in the U.S. prison system
- Strategies for improving the lives of women in prison

STEP FOUR (optional): Ask each small group to choose one strategy from the list, research how it might be implemented in the community, state, or country, and present their findings to the rest of the class. To get started, refer to "Ten Ways to Learn More About Women in Prison," in the appendix to *Inside This Place, Not of It* (p. 270).

STEP FIVE (optional): Send (or email) your letters to Voice of Witness, where they will be forwarded to the organization Justice Now, our *Inside This Place, Not of It* book partners. Justice Now supports many of the women whose narratives appear in the book.

> Voice of Witness
> 849 Valencia Street
> San Francisco, CA 94110
> Attn: Education Program
> Email: cliff.mayotte@voiceofwitness.org

POSSIBLE ORAL HISTORY PROJECT: Class creates an oral history project focusing on gender bias in their school community. Students craft interview questions based on their work in the Body Stories unit and interview classmates, friends, and school faculty and staff.

MEDIA OPTION: Organizational Website: **The Beat Within: A Weekly Publication of Writing and Art From the Inside.** Based in San Francisco, the Beat Within's mission is to provide incarcerated youth with a consistent opportunity to share their ideas and life experiences in a safe space that encourages literacy, self-expression, some critical thinking skills, and healthy, supportive relationships with adults and their community. *beatwithin.org*

VICTIMS, SURVIVORS AND CRIMINALS:
INSIDE THIS PLACE, NOT OF IT

TIME NEEDED: Five class periods.

MATERIALS: *Inside This Place, Not of It*, Station handouts, string, tape measure or yardstick, Satellites Handout, paper, pens, large pieces of butcher paper or poster-size sticky notes.

OBJECTIVE: Using narratives from *Inside This Place Not Of It*, students analyze and explore the challenges faced by women in prison while addressing larger issues within the U.S criminal justice system.

RELATED CORE CURRICULAR STANDARDS: Reading History RH.9–10.1. RH.9–10.2. Speaking and Listening SL.9–10.1. Writing W.9–10.2.

CONNECTIONS: This unit can be adapted for use with narratives from *Surviving Justice*. Other narratives from *Inside This Place, Not of It* can be substituted for the ones suggested below.

OVERVIEW

This unit explores the realities of women in U.S. prisons. It allows students to analyze and personalize the experiences of incarcerated women as they examine the labels "criminal," "victim," and "survivor."

NARRATIVE EXCERPT: "After just coming out of a relationship where I'd fought for my life, I began fighting for my life again in the judicial system. I don't believe the system handled my case fairly. I had neighbors testifying for me, I had family members testifying for me, I had police reports, I had medical records, but none of that meant anything to the prosecutor. Their job was just to convict me, it was like a show. The prosecutor was trying for a sentence of thirty years to life. I had to fight to not go into a prison for life." —*Sheri Dwight*

ESSENTIAL QUESTIONS:

- *What does it mean to be a criminal?*
- *What does it mean to be a victim?*
- *What does it mean to be a survivor?*
- *How do some people transform struggles into sources of strength?*

PREPARATION: Devise a system for dividing students into groups and assigning appropriate readings. The creation of the groups should be informed by efforts to solicit a diversity of perspectives and ways in which members can contribute to their group.

STEP ONE: The activities during the first day of the unit focus primarily on activating prior student knowledge of the issue. Have students do a "pair-share" in which they discuss the following questions (5 minutes):

- *If you had to spend the next eight years in jail, what would you miss the most?*
- *If you had to spend the rest of your life in jail, what would be the biggest challenges you would face?*

STEP TWO: Introduce students to *Inside This Place, Not of It.* Provide a brief overview of the book and the manner by which women's stories were documented (5 minutes).

STEP THREE: Create a KWL chart for student reflection (or make a copy of the chart, found on page 45). The chart should be readily accessible, as students will revisit it during the course of the unit. This activity will give students an opportunity to activate prior knowledge and reveal assumptions they may have about women in prison. Conclude the activity by asking students what they would like to learn about women in prison (10 minutes).

STEP FOUR: Divide the class into four groups. (These groups may or may not correlate with the reading groups students will use for the remainder of the unit.) For larger class sizes, divide the class into eight groups and simply reproduce each station twice. Inform groups that they will rotate through four stations spread throughout the classroom. Provide students with instructions as to when they need to rotate. Each station will have a unique prompt and set of instructions. Students will record their insights for each activity on the *Inside This Place, Not of It* Stations handout (35 minutes).

STATION ONE: YOUR NEW HOME

Housing more inmates in a cell than what it is designed for is common in the U.S. and anywhere else overcrowding is present. The average prison cell built today is at least 70 square feet (7x11 or 8x9), but only about 60 square feet are usable, resulting in 30 square feet per prisoner if double celled. Some older prison and jail cells provide 40 to 56 square feet (5x8 or 7x8). Federal judges in many states have ruled since 1977 that every prisoner deserves at least 60 square feet of cell space. The fact is that cell size varies depending upon the type of facility. —Institutional Corrections, *a report by Mark Stevens, Assistant Professor of Criminology, California State University, Fresno, 2004*

DIRECTIONS

Create a prison cell using the string and measuring tools provided. Your group's cell must be at least seventy but no more than ninety square feet.

Once you have constructed your cell, reflect on the questions below and record your insights on your *Inside This Place, Not of It* Stations handout.

- *What are the dimensions of your cell?*
- *How many square feet does it contain (multiply its length by its width)?*
- *What challenges would you face living in such a small space and sharing it with another person?*

STATION TWO: RISING NUMBERS

Though women make up only a small minority of the prison and jail population, slightly less than 7 percent, their numbers are increasing at rates that far surpass men. In 1977, 11,212 women were in prison. As of 2007, that number had increased to 107,000. The number of women in prison has grown dramatically since the 1980s due to several factors: mandatory minimum sentencing for drug crimes which preclude judicial discretion, the dismantling of the U.S. mental health system, and increased prosecution of "survival" crimes, which include check forgery and minor embezzlement. Over the last four decades, hundreds of thousands of women have been sentenced to jail and prison for nonviolent and first-time offenses, for offenses that arise from drug addiction or mental health problems, or as a result of minor involvement in offenses perpetrated by their husbands or boyfriends. —*Inside This Place, Not of It*, Introduction

DIRECTIONS

Discuss the questions on the next page with your fellow group members. Then, record your group's insights using your *Inside This Place, Not of It* Stations handout.

- *How might the "dismantling of the U.S. mental health system" increase the number of people in prison?*
- *Based on its context in the passage, what are "survival crimes"?*
- *Would you ever commit a survival crime? Why or why not?*

STATION THREE: GENDER AND THE PRISON SYSTEM

"Because women are a minority in the prison system, they face particular challenges. A prison healthcare system designed for men that mandates, for example, shackling during transportation to and from the hospital, suddenly rises from the unpleasant to the horrific when the transported prisoner shackled at the ankles is a woman in the late stages of active labor, as experienced by Olivia Hamilton"

—*Inside This Place, Not of It*, Introduction

DIRECTIONS

With your fellow group members, reflect on the similarities and differences in the challenges men and women face in prison. Record your group's insights using the Venn diagram on your *Inside This Place, Not of It* Stations handout.

STATION FOUR: LIFE AFTER PRISON

DIRECTIONS

Briefly discuss with your group members the challenges people face once they are released from prison.

Then, using your *Inside This Place, Not of It* Stations handout, create a drawing or cartoon that illustrates an example of one of these challenges.

For additional ideas regarding challenges people face after being released from prison, you may want to consult Appendix VII: Post-Prison Consequences pp. 250–254 of *Inside This Place, Not of It*.

INSIDE THIS PLACE, NOT OF IT: STATIONS

STATION ONE: YOUR NEW HOME

- What are the dimensions of your cell?

- How many square feet does it contain (multiply its length by its width)?

- What challenges would you face living in such a small space and sharing it with another person?

STATION TWO: RISING NUMBERS

- How might the "dismantling of the U.S. mental health system" increase the number of people in prison?

- Based on its context in the passage, what are "survival crimes"?

- Would you ever commit a survival crime? Why or why not?

STATION THREE: GENDER AND THE PRISON SYSTEM

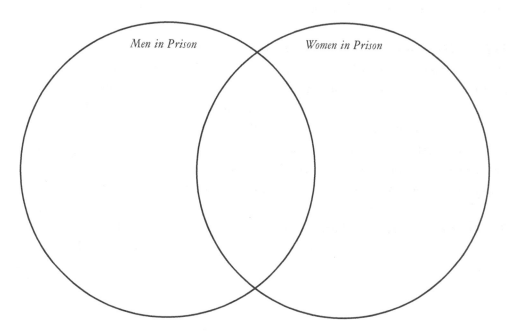

STATION FOUR: LIFE AFTER PRISON
(Create your drawing or cartoon on the back.)

STEP FIVE: Revisit the KWL chart and ask students to add to the "Want to Learn" and "Learned" sections of the chart (5 minutes).

DAY TWO

STEP ONE: As a writing warm-up, ask students to reflect on the following question (5 minutes):

- *"What is a criminal?"*

STEP TWO: In a "pair-share," students share their ideas with a partner and then discuss the following questions (5 minutes):

- *How are your ideas similar?*
- *How do they differ?*

STEP THREE: Working in their groups from the previous day, students read pp. 39–44 of Sheri Dwight's narrative (20 minutes). Groups can read aloud, or silently, using the Talk to the Text (p. 23) activity or reading strategies listed on p. 124. As students are reading, ask them to make a list of people who have had a major impact on Sheri's life—her parents, her children, her husband, etc. Around each person's name, students respond to the prompts below. Encourage them to add to their initial insights as they continue to read.

- *Describe Sheri's relationship with this person or these people.*
- *What happens because of this relationship?*

STEP FOUR: Conclude the activity by asking students to share their insights. This can be done as a class, in groups, or with partners (5 minutes).

STEP FIVE: Each (already established) group will be assigned one of the following four narratives from *Inside This Place Not of It:* Teri Hancock (15 pp.), Emily Madison (16 pp.), Taisie Baldwin (12 pp.), Irma Rodriguez (12 pp.). During this "Independent Practice" reading session, students can read independently, with a partner, or with the entire group (15 minutes). Similar to the earlier reading activity, as students read this story they will reflect on people who have had a substantial impact on their narrator's life. Remind students to include people that played a major role in the narrator's life before, during, and—when applicable—after her time in prison. Any reading and reflections that students do not complete during class time become homework.

STEP SIX: Revisit the KWL chart introduced on the first day of the unit. For items not yet addressed in the "Want to Learn" section, discuss how the class will work to include them in the days ahead (5 minutes).

STEP ONE: As a warm-up activity, students do a "pair-share" for the following question (5 minutes):

- *What are prisons for?*

STEP TWO: As a class, discuss themes that surfaced in the passages from Sheri Dwight's narrative that students read during the previous class period (7–10 minutes). Students may find it helpful to have a working definition of themes:

"A unifying or dominant idea in a speech, work of literature, film, etc."

Examples from Sheri Dwight's narrative may include *abuse, fear, injustice, survival*, and *violence.*

STEP THREE: Introduce *Inside This Place, Not of It* Theme Satellites. This activity will enable students to record quotes and details that support the development of themes from narratives in the book. As a class, complete several sample Theme Satellites that identify themes that developed in Sheri Dwight's story (10 minutes).

INSIDE THIS PLACE, NOT OF IT
THEME SATELLITE EXAMPLE SHEET

1. On a separate piece of paper, using the example below, draw four bubbles, each containing a theme from *Inside This Place, Not of It*.
2. Around each bubble, draw three boxes and connect them to your theme bubble with lines.
3. In each example box, provide a quote and/or a description of a detail from the story that shows this theme.
4. At least one of these examples must include a quote from the text that shows this theme.
5. Include the relevant page number(s) with any quotes you use.

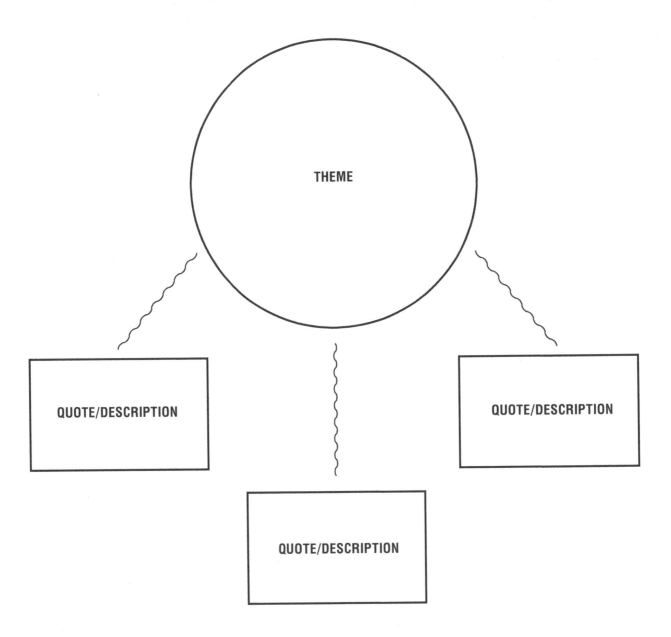

STEP FOUR: Students work with a partner from their group to complete the *Inside This Place, Not of It* Theme Satellites graphic organizer for the story they have read (20 minutes).

STEP FIVE: Students discuss the following questions in their groups (10 minutes).

- *What is justice?*
- *What is injustice?*
- *Can justice lead to injustice? If so, how?*

STEP SIX: Revisit the KWL chart. For items not yet addressed in the "Want to Learn" section, discuss how the class will work to include them in the days ahead (5 minutes).

DAY FOUR

NOTES: The Introduction to Dialectical Reading Journals handout (found on page 138) is designed to provide students with an overview of reading journals. This lesson operates under the assumption that students have experience using some type of reading journal with which they apply active reading strategies (listed on page 137). If students have not yet used a reading journal, consider facilitating a separate lesson on how to use a journal to employ active reading strategies.

STEP ONE: As a warm-up activity, ask students to reflect in writing on the following question (5 minutes):

- *Do you think society treats people differently if they have spent time in prison?*

STEP TWO: Students share their ideas with a partner and then discuss the following questions (5 minutes):

- *How are your ideas similar?*
- *How do they differ?*

STEP THREE: Divide students into their narrative groups. Assign groups one of the following narratives from *Inside This Place, Not of It*: Olivia Hamilton (13 pp.), Francesca Salavieri (14 pp.), Marilyn Sanderson (13 pp.), and Charlie Morningstar (16 pp.). Provide students with the opportunity to read independently or with a partner.

Students will employ active reading strategies by using the Dialectical Reading Journal handout on page 138 of the Educator Resources section. Any reading not completed in class will be done as homework (35 minutes).

STEP FOUR: As a class, conclude the period by briefly discussing the following questions (5 minutes):

- *What is important to the narrator of your story?*
- *Has prison changed what this person considers important to her? If so, how?*

STEP ONE: As a warm-up activity, ask students to work with a partner to create a Prisoner's Bill of Rights. Imagine that it will be used to inform the policies, procedures, and facilities of future prisons constructed in your state (10 minutes).

STEP TWO: Students will collaborate with their groups to create a "Life Map" for their narrator (30 minutes). Their Life Maps should include the following items:

- A drawing of the narrator.
- A summary of the narrator's life before, during, and—when applicable—after prison. Remind students that a good summary often includes information that addresses the *who, what, when, where, why,* and *how* questions.
- An explanation of themes that developed throughout the narrator's story and the details that helped create these themes.
- A drawing to accompany each theme.

STEP THREE: Groups will hang their completed Life Maps in the classroom. Students should do a "gallery walk" tour of the room to examine their classmates' ideas (5–7 minutes).

STEP FOUR: Unit concludes by revisiting the KWL chart. For items that have not been addressed in the "Want to Learn" section, discuss ways in which students or the class as a whole can pursue future learning opportunities (5 minutes).

POSSIBLE ORAL HISTORY PROJECT: Class creates an oral history project using the discussion questions of the unit, the writing /discussion prompts, and the Prisoner's Bill of Rights to craft interview questions for an exploration of gender isssues within in the U.S. criminal justice system and beyond. Students can interview friends, family, teachers, and members of the community.

MEDIA OPTION: *Voices Project / Public Secrets*: *Public Secrets* is an interactive testimonial in which women incarcerated in the California State Prison System reveal the secrets of the war on drugs, the criminal justice system, and the prison industrial complex. *Public Secrets* was developed in collaboration with Justice Now and with the support of Vectors: Journal of Culture and Technology in a Dynamic Vernacular. This project contains strong language and graphic descriptions of prison conditions. (*vectors.usc.edu/issues/4/publicsecrets/*)

HURRICANE KATRINA: RACE, CLASS, AND DEMOCRACY IN THE UNITED STATES

OVERVIEW

Hurricane Katrina and its aftermath provide an opportunity to examine race and class in contemporary American society as they are both perceived and acted upon. The narratives from *Voices From the Storm: The People of New Orleans on Hurricane Katrina and Its Aftermath* offer a ground's-eye view of what many citizens experienced during Hurricane Katrina, and these lessons provide a multifaceted exploration of the perceptions and realities of American democracy.

HURRICANE KATRINA: CRITICAL READING LOG

TIME NEEDED: One to two class periods or homework assignments.

MATERIALS: *Voices from the Storm*, and Critical Reading Log format.

OBJECTIVE: Using first-person narrative to build reading comprehension and critical thinking skills through personal student reflection.

RELATED CORE CURRICULUM STANDARDS: Reading History RH.9–10.2. RH.9–10.4 RH.9–10.10. Writing W.9–10.1.

CONNECTIONS: This activity can be done with any narrative from *Voices From the Storm* and the other books in the Voice of Witness series.

NARRATIVE EXCERPT: "Everybody in the Ninth Ward, down in that Desire project, where a brother used to rock at, that's where all the water was. Back there where I live at, it's through, it's finished. You got a lot of people back there, man, already really didn't have nothin', you know? People back there scufflin' to keep the little bit they got. All they got now, as far as the black poor people are concerned back there, is uncertainty. And mildew, they got plenty of that out there. They ain't got nothing but poor black people out there, gettin' the stuff out their houses, breathing in toxins. That's real. That's real, man." —*Anthony Letcher*

Note: All information for this activity should be entered in the Critical Thinking Log.

STEP ONE: Read Introduction to *Voices from the Storm* (4 pp.) and the narrative of Anthony Letcher from all four parts of the book (16 pp.). Encourage students to use active reading strategies (35–40 minutes).

STEP TWO: Have students write a 150-word summary of the people and/or events that occurred in the passage (20 minutes).

STEP THREE: Have students select two **quotations** from the reading that they feel are important or interesting and briefly explain why they chose each quotation (10 minutes).

STEP FOUR: Encourage students to make a connection between what they read and something they have seen, experienced, heard, or read about. What did it remind them of? Why is this story/account important? Have students write about both parts of the connection—something specific from the oral history narrative, and something specific from outside the narrative (10–12 minutes).

STEP FIVE: Have students create three to five oral history questions they would ask Anthony Letcher if they were to conduct an oral history interview with him. Strive to "find the holes" in the story and ask questions that could help students better understand his story/experience (7–10 minutes).

CRITICAL READING LOG FORMAT

NAME: **CLASS/PERIOD:**   **DATE:**

TITLE OF BOOK/STORY:

AUTHOR:

SUMMARY:

QUOTATION:

EXPLANATION OF QUOTATION:

CONNECTION/REFLECTIONS:

ORAL HISTORY QUESTIONS:

STEP SIX (optional): Students do a "pair-share" with their reading logs, comparing quotes, connections, and oral history questions (7–10 minutes).

POSSIBLE ORAL HISTORY PROJECT: Create an oral history project using the Critical Reading Log format, with student-written biographies as the "text."

MEDIA OPTION: Podcasts from Youth Radio/Open Society Foundations: **Generation Katrina: Youth Voices from New Orleans** (*www.soros.org/resources/multimedia/katrina/projects/GenKatrina/story_GenKatrina.php*). A one-hour collection of personal narratives documenting the world of young people in New Orleans after Katrina.

HURRICANE KATRINA: PERCEPTIONS
AND REALITIES OF CLASS, RACE, AND DEMOCRACY

TIME NEEDED: Three to four days (5-day version available on Voice of Witness website)

MATERIALS: *Voices from the Storm*, large pieces of paper or poster-size sticky notes, markers, handouts, and background information/images on Hurricane Katrina and New Orleans.

OBJECTIVE: Explore perceptions of class, race, and democracy through an examination of Hurricane Katrina and multiple first-person narratives from *Voices from the Storm*.

RELATED CURRICULAR STANDARDS: Reading History RH.9–10.1, RH.11–12.1, RH.9–10.2, RH.11–12.2, RH.9–10.6, RH.11–12.6, RH.9–10.9, RH.11–12.9. Writing W.9–10.1, W.11–12.1, W.9–10.2, W.11–12.2, W.9–10.7, W.11–12.7, SL.9–10.1. Speaking and Listening SL.11–12.1, SL.9–10.4, SL.11–12.4.

CONNECTIONS: Worksheets for this lesson can be adapted and used for other narratives in the Voice of Witness series.

NARRATIVE EXCERPT: "Katrina was truly a disaster, but for me Katrina was a blessing 'cause it turned my life around. I've been wanting to leave New Orleans. You're not treated right in New Orleans, you're not treated fair. New Orleans is the city that forgot to care, and the city that care had forgotten about. You hear about the big easy, you hear about carnival. But man, we go through hell in New Orleans." —*Patricia Thompson*

ESSENTIAL QUESTIONS:

- *How does perception impact identity?*
- *How did racial and class divisions impact the national response to Katrina?*
- *How did the events of Katrina challenge our democratic ideals?*

OVERVIEW

Hurricane Katrina and its aftermath provide an opportunity to examine race and class in contemporary American society as they are both perceived and acted upon. These lessons first encourage students to consider their perceptions of their own selves in relation to the rest of the world, and then to apply those differences to the catastrophe in New Orleans. Before Katrina, the perceptions New Orleans residents had of themselves, their city, and their government were informed by racial and class divisions, though largely unspoken or explicit. After the storm, these divisions became glaringly apparent and were also echoed and distorted in the media coverage of the disaster.

DAY ONE

STEP ONE: Set up poster activity, entitled Perceptions of My Community, as warm-up for the lessons/ readings that follow. It is an opportunity for students to reflect on the many sources that shape perceptions in their community. If desired, have students reflect on the following prompts in writing for a few minutes before beginning the activity.

Hang four pieces of large poster board or large sticky notes around the room. On each poster write the following half sentences:

- (Your neighborhood, town, or city) is _____
- People from (your neighborhood, town, or city) are_____
- Being from (your neighborhood, town, or city) means_____
- Young people in (your neighborhood, town, or City) _____

Students then circulate around the room and finish each sentence according to their perceptions of their community. They should write at least one response for all four prompts (7-10 minutes).

STEP TWO: Students then do a "gallery walk" to examine all the completed sentences (5 minutes).

STEP THREE: At the conclusion of the "gallery walk," students identify the top three themes/ perceptions from each poster. The class then charts the positive, negative, and neutral perceptions. At the conclusion of this activity, discuss the following question (15 minutes).

- *Where do the perceptions of our community come from?*

Make a list of the sources (family, friends, internet, television, etc.).

STEP FOUR: Before providing students with necessary background information on Hurricane Katrina, create a slightly altered version of the KWL activity for the class using the chart provided. This chart should be centrally located in the classroom and used throughout the unit for student questions and responses.

WHAT I HAVE HEARD AND SEEN	WHAT I HAVE COME TO BELIEVE	WHAT I WANT TO KNOW

STEP FIVE: The remainder of the class period should be spent going over background material (maps, time lines, reports) on Hurricane Katrina and New Orleans from the appendices of *Voices from the Storm* (p. 261). Use the student questions from the KWL chart and the community perceptions from the Poster Activity to frame and share information. (15–20 minutes).

STEP SIX (for homework): Create reading groups for the following suggested narratives from *Voices from the Storm*:

- Patricia Thompson
- Dan Bright
- Father Vien The Nguyen
- Renee Martin
- Abdulrahman Zeitoun

Ask students to read the intro and the story of their assigned individual. If students need additional time to read, use some time at the beginning of the next class period. Students should do the Talk to the Text activity or incorporate other active reading strategies.

DAY TWO

STEP ONE: Additional reading time, if needed (10–15 minutes).

STEP TWO: Warm-up activity: Four Corners (5 minutes):

In each corner of the room, hang one of the following signs: **strongly agree, agree, disagree, strongly disagree.** Then give the following instructions:

"We'll be doing an activity in which you will be moving around the classroom, stating your opinion and supporting your point of view. Bring your warm-up paper with you.

I'll be reading the statements from the warm-up. After I read the statement, stand in the corner of the room under the sign that represents your opinion—strongly agree, agree, disagree, or strongly disagree. After you move there, I'll be asking different people in that opinion group to back up their opinions with explanations."

Depending on schedules and engagement, this activity can take longer and be even richer (10 minutes).

STEP THREE: EXPERT GROUPS
In groups, students work together, but each fill in a worksheet on the individual assigned to them. Make sure to note the difference between questions 1 and 2 (20 minutes).

STEP FOUR: PRESENTATION CHARTS
During the next class period, groups will be making short presentations on their assigned narrators. In preparation for this, give each group a Presentation Chart that they will fill out for their presentations. With any remaining class time, groups can begin writing responses on their charts (5–10 minutes).

VOICES FROM THE STORM

———————

Read each of the following statements. On your own piece of paper, write whether you agree or disagree with the statement, then write a sentence explaining your opinion. You do not need to copy the statements on your paper:

1. If a *huge natural disaster* were to hit (*your city or town*) tomorrow, the city would be prepared to handle it.

2. If a *huge natural disaster* were to hit (*your city or town*) tomorrow, my family would be prepared.

3. City, state, and federal government should be responsible for helping people deal with natural disasters.

4. The government helps all people equally when it comes to things like natural disasters.

5. In a natural disaster, prisoners and undocumented immigrants do not deserve the same assistance from the government as other people do.

EXPERT GROUP WORKSHEET

While talking with other students who studied the same Katrina story as the one you read, fill in this chart to better understand the narrator's experiences.

NAME OF THE PERSON YOU STUDIED:
LOCATION IN NEW ORLEANS BEFORE KATRINA:

LIFE BEFORE THE STORM

1. What are three ways you can describe this person's personality? Give evidence for each description.

   -
   -
   -

2. What are three ways you can describe this person's life before the storm? Give evidence for each description.

   -
   -
   -

3. What are their perceptions of New Orleans? What do they say about living there? Give evidence for each description.

THE STORM

4. Describe this person's situation as the storm approached/hit New Orleans. Where was he or she? With whom? How did he/she feel about the storm? Why was he or she still in the city? *(You may not have a lot of information for this one, depending on which person's story you are studying.)*

5. Identify three major things that happened to this person or that this person did after the levees broke (the morning of Monday, August 29) and in the following days (through September 4). Include locations, if you can.

    •
    •
    •

6. How did this person respond to those events? What was his or her state of mind?

THE WEEK AFTER/WEEKS AFTER THE STORM

7. What was life like for your narrator during the weeks after the storm? Where was he or she? Why?

8. How did this person respond to these weeks? What was his or her state of mind? How was he or she adapting to his or her environment?

LOOKING BACK

9. Where is the person you studied living at this point? How does he or she feel about living in New Orleans? How have his or her perceptions of New Orleans been challenged?

10. Looking back, how does the person you studied seem the same and/or different because of his or her Katrina experiences? How does your person view life now?

MODEL FOR PRESENTATION CHART

NAME OF THE PERSON STUDIED:

LOCATION IN NEW ORLEANS BEFORE KATRINA:

LIFE BEFORE THE STORM

_____ *was like:*	_____ *'s life was like:*

THE STORM

Highlights from _____ 's experiences during the storm and after the levees broke:	*Descriptions of _____ 's state of mind during the storm and after the levees broke:*

THE WEEK AFTER/WEEKS AFTER THE STORM

Highlights after the storm—write your person's location and state of mind.

LOOKING BACK

Highlight—where is your person now? How has his or her life changed?

GOLDEN DESCRIPTION

What is the one story the rest of the class needs to know about the person you studied? If you could only describe his or her experiences in two sentences, what would they be?

STEP FIVE: For homework, students write reflections of the following questions (one page):

- *What in the Katrina stories surprised you?*
- *What is most important to you in the stories you read and heard?*
- *How do you think these people's situations could have been improved?*
- *Other than the hurricane itself, what other factors contributed to their struggles?*

DAY THREE

STEP ONE: Students pair up and share written reflection answers. Each pair then shares their answers with the class. Students should be encouraged to use direct quotes from their reading. (10 minutes)

After a short "gallery walk," allow students to share their responses to the activity using New Orleans as a model. Consider the following questions:

- *Have your perceptions of New Orleans changed as a result of your reading?*
- *In your opinion, what are the sources that have shaped perceptions of New Orleans?*

STEP TWO: Groups finish their Expert Worksheets and Presentation Chart from the previous day. (10 minutes).

STEP THREE: Each group presents basic info on their assigned narrator while the rest of the class takes notes on the Presentation Note-Taker Worksheet for comparing experiences. As presentations unfold, the teacher asks groups probing questions, elicits comments/questions from class members, and pulls out comparisons from class members. Students incorporate responses from their Note-Taker Worksheets. (30 minutes).

NOTE-TAKER WORKSHEETS

As each group presents a little bit of the story of the person they studied, fill in the chart. In the left-hand column, write how that person and his or her experiences during Katrina were similar to the person you studied. In the right-hand column, write how that person and his or her experiences were different from the person you studied. Cross out the chart for the person you studied.

	Similarities to your person	Differences from your person
PATRICIA THOMPSON		

	Similarities to your person	Differences from your person
RENEE MARTIN		

	Similarities to your person	Differences from your person
DAN BRIGHT		

	Similarities to your person	Differences from your person
ABDULRAHMAN ZEITOUN		

	Similarities to your person	Differences from your person
FATHER VIEN THE NGUYEN		

STEP FOUR: Students revisit the KWL chart—adding to the W and L sections, in addition to repeating the first step of the Poster Activity (on paper or whiteboard), with the following changes (10 minutes):

- New Orleans is _____
- People from New Orleans are_____
- Being from New Orleans means_____

Consider the following question:

- Have your perceptions of New Orleans changed as a result of your reading? In what ways?

POSSIBLE ORAL HISTORY PROJECT: Class creates an oral history project exploring local examples that reflect perceptions and realities of race, class, and democracy. Project could also have an environmental justice framework, collecting stories from a variety of individuals in the community.

MEDIA OPTION: Documentary Films:

When the Levees Broke (dir. Spike Lee) HBO Films, 2006 (*www.hbo.com/documentaries/when-the-levees-broke-a-requiem-in-four-acts/index.html*)

Trouble the Water (dirs. Tia Lessin and Carl Deal). Elsewhere Films, 2008 (*www.troublethewaterfilm.com*)

FIELD GUIDE TO CONDUCTING ORAL HISTORY

OVERVIEW

Part 3 serves as the Voice of Witness "field guide" to conducting oral histories and creating oral history projects with students. Beginning with time lines and checklists and ending with examples of "amplified" oral history projects, it covers every step of the process. Through conducting their own oral histories and opening themselves to the untold stories in their communities, students create an experiential and civically engaged relationship to history—*doing* history as opposed to just learning about it.

PROJECT TIME LINE AND CHECKLIST

The time it takes to complete an oral history project can vary greatly. It can be done as a single five-week unit, or it can be part of a larger, integrated project or service learning opportunity that can last an entire semester. The following time line reflects an approach that takes five to six weeks. It is meant as a guideline and not a script. Depending on schedules, student needs, and curriculum, teachers can expand or contract the time line as needed or desired.

PHASE 1: INTRODUCTION AND CONTEXT
Two to three class periods
- Introduce oral history
  - Choose narratives to read and discuss
- Discuss how to conduct interviews (interview questions, recording devices, etc).
  - Practice interviews with each other—in pairs and "modeling."

PHASE 2: FORMULATING PROJECTS
One class period
- Discuss topics/issues that are related to class curriculum.
- Discuss project goals. Get specific about what projects/interviews will look like and what will they cover.
  - Who will tell a great story?
  - How will this be recorded?
  - How will this be edited/compiled into a final product?

PHASE 3: THE INTERVIEW
One to two weeks
- Make a list of possible interviewees and start making contact with them. Make sure you have a backup in case the best options fall through.
- Set up a time for interviews.
- Solidify your interview questions.
- Interview.

PHASE 4: DEBRIEF, LOGISTICS, AND LISTENING

1-2 class periods

- After the interview(s), take a preliminary look at the material and think about how the interview satisfied the goals for the project set up in Phase 2.
  - Will a follow-up interview be necessary?
  - Will an entirely different interview be necessary?

PHASE 5: TRANSCRIBING, EDITING, AND PROOFING

One to two weeks

- Transcription
- Editing and shaping the interview into a narrative
- Proofing and final edits

PHASE 6: SHARING YOUR ORAL HISTORIES

Two to three class periods

- Final edits, uploading, etc.
- Presentation logistics (planning, invitations, etc.)
- Community presentation
- Reflection/assessment

ORAL HISTORY PLANNING SHEET AND CHECKLIST

Oral history projects require a fair amount of planning and logistics. The following planning sheet and checklist can be handed out to students to help them stay organized and on task during their project.

ORAL HISTORY PLANNING SHEET

Choice 1 name:	Why would this person be good to interview?
Choice 2 name:	
What do you think will be hard about this interview?	
What are you going to do to make it easier?	

- Do you have a recording device you can use to conduct your interview, or will you need to borrow one?

Tonight, talk to one of the people you would like to interview, and write down dates and times during which you could conduct your interview. Plan for about an hour to set up for and conduct an interview.

	Date:	Time:	Place:
Interview option 1:			
Interview option 2:			
Interview option 3:			

- The next time our class meets, you will make a schedule with classmates so that each of you will get adequate time with the recorders.

ORAL HISTORY PROJECT CHECKLIST

	Decide who you will interview
	Write questions to guide your interview
	Conduct your interview
	Transcribe your interview
	Brainstorm follow-up questions
	Follow-up interview
	Add to your transcript
	Select the best stories (with a yellow highlighter)
	Proofread your selections
	Clarify with brackets
	Peer edit (more than one student)
	Adult/teacher edit: do you need a few more follow-up questions?
	(Reinterview)
	(Type responses right into first draft)
	Print out draft (with reinterview info, if necessary) and take to interviewee for fact-checking
	One more adult/teacher edit
	Save as final draft
	Print final draft and hand in recording, transcript, and final draft

PREPARING FOR YOUR
ORAL HISTORY PROJECT

ETHICS AND PRACTICALITIES

ETHICS

A major component of the Voice of Witness Framework of Oral History is to honor people and their stories. There are ethical (and legal) considerations to discuss with students before conducting oral history interviews. This section will cover basic Voice of Witness principles, guidelines, and practicalities of conducting oral history. For additional material on the topic, see the Oral History Association's website (*www.oralhistory.org*) for an extensive list of guidelines.

SEEK OUT NARRATORS WHO ARE ENTHUSIASTIC ABOUT TELLING THEIR STORY

A student may really want to interview someone because they are certain that person has amazing stories to tell, but if that individual is ambivalent or reluctant about being interviewed, students must respect that. Cajoling and pleading is not okay.

When selecting potential narrators for an oral history project, it is essential to remember that everyone has a story and that an "unamplified" voice does not have to be someone who has been victimized or is suffering through a crisis. Voice of Witness cofounder Lola Vollen describes this as "celebrating the rich tapestry of everyday voices." While there is no need to shy away from stories of struggle or adversity, seeking narrators solely on the basis of "victim stories" can create an unnecessary burden for both narrator and interviewer, putting students in an ethically compromised position of ignoring deserving stories.

Narrators in the Voice of Witness book series share their stories related to human rights abuses, but these narratives also contain many other aspects of the narrators' lives. While students are contemplating potential narrators, encourage them to be interested in the "whole person," which will enable them to create a multifaceted oral history portrait of their narrators.

RELEASE FORM

All narrators must read and sign a release form before their interview. The release form is permission in writing for the interview and states that the subject understands and agrees to the use of her or his edited interview for publication, broadcast, performance, or public presentation. This is not just a courtesy but also a legal and ethical obligation. In some cases, when a signed release form is not possible, narrators can have the release form read to them and verbally agree. This verbal agreement should be recorded and saved with the audio file of the narrator's interview. The sample release form below can be adapted to suit your school or community.

SAMPLE RELEASE FORM

I, _____ (full name) hereby give permission for Voice of Witness to record, transcribe, and consider this interview for publication.

I understand that I have complete control over how my interview can be used, and can choose to remain anonymous if the interview is used in any form. (This includes, and is not limited to, text or audio excerpts of the interview in newspapers, magazines, and the internet.)

I will receive a transcript and/or recording of my interview from Voice of Witness for my personal use upon my request.

Voice of Witness will not publish anything without my consent, and will do everything to protect my privacy. They will not share my identity or personal information with anyone else.

If I do not speak English, I will be provided with an interpreter who will explain this consent form in my language.

_____
Signature

_____
Date

_____
Address

_____
City, State, Zip

_____
Phone #

_____
Other way of getting in contact

THE CHAIN OF TRUST

When preparing to find narrators for books in the Voice of Witness series, the organization employs an approach called the "Chain of Trust." Used by Just Associates and writer/Voice of Witness editor Annie Holmes, the Chain of Trust links trusted service and advocacy organizations to potential narrators. By working through these organizations, oral historians can develop relationships with narrators in an ethical, respectful way. Teachers and students can employ this method by reaching out to community organizations when in the planning stages of an oral history project.

ORAL HISTORY AS COMMUNITY SERVICE LEARNING

More often than not, oral history projects are designed to be community projects. Oral history programming and curriculum enhance immersion experiences and community service learning for students, deepening a social justice consciousness of their communities. When students interview members of their community, they can engage those who need to tell their story. These are stories that have a significant place in history, current events, and the cultural landscape of a community. If the final project culminates in a public sharing, the people who are interviewed are publicly honored. When students create this kind of meaningful work for their community, they act as "upstanders" and participate in community building, invoking social awareness and positive change.

From the moment an oral history project begins, everything from brainstorming with students about the reasons for conducting oral history to the final stage of presentation or performance becomes an exercise in community building. Many projects choose to focus upon a particular period in history or center around a particular theme, community issue, or event. Other projects can allow for more open-ended approaches for students to discover their own individual themes and narrators.

CONTACTING YOUR POTENTIAL NARRATOR

For some students, contacting the person they would like to interview can be a daunting task, especially if the potential narrator is not already an acquaintance of the student. Remind students that people will most likely be interested in what they are doing, but that they will have to explain themselves fully. Of course, being courteous is important, and the more clearly students can describe their project, the better. The following is a brief example of one way to have a respectful first encounter with a potential narrator a student has not previously met.

Student: *Hi, my name is_____ and I'm a student at _____ School. I'm participating in an oral history project and I'm looking for individuals who might be willing to share their stories or experiences about the _____ event or other experiences with_____ . I heard Ms._____ might know a lot about that. Might she be available to talk with me?*

Person: *Yes, that's me. I'm happy to talk. Can you tell me a little more about this project?*

Student: *I'd be happy to. It's an oral history project where each member of our class is finding someone in their community whom they think have an unheard story to tell. The focus of the project is on _____ and I thought you would be a good person to talk with because _____ and _____. If you wouldn't mind sitting down with me, I'd like to interview you for about half an hour on your experience doing _____. I will have a set of questions and all you will have to do is answer them.*

Person: *Sure, I don't see why not.*

Student: *Great! When is a good time for you?*

Then set up a time that works for both people at a place that will be both comfortable and convenient. Make sure you give the person your contact information in case they need to reschedule. Also, before you hang up, ask the person for a brief bit of biographical information (age, place of residence, school attended, etc.) so that you will know a bit about them before going into the interview.

Students need to be flexible and willing to balance both patience and persistence when attempting to make a connection with a narrator. If they do not hear back from their message, email, or text within four to six days, they should try again. Expect that this part of the process will take time. It's a very good idea for students to have several potential narrators on their list in case one falls through. Below is a handout for students to use as a reference when they are contacting potential narrators.

NARRATOR CONTACT CHECKLIST

When first making contact with potential narrators, you should ask them the following:

- What is their contact information: full name, telephone number, and email address?
- Would they mind being recorded via an audio or video recorder?
- Are they able to come to the school or meet off campus?
- What are good dates and times for the interview?
- What is the best way to follow up with them after the interview?

Record these details and submit them to your teacher for approval.

PHONE CALLS: Before you call, role play with a partner (who "answers" the call), stating your name, what school/neighborhood group you are with, the goal of the project and how they might be able to participate/how you need their help. Then, make the real call. If you need to leave a message, speak slowly and clearly, and leave your contact email or cell phone number twice.

EMAIL: Clearly state who you are, which organization/school you are from, and what the goals and intentions are for your project. If you have links to your school be sure to include those. Have another person proofread the message before you send it.

FOLLOW-THROUGH: Sometimes people will need more than one email or phone call. Be persistent, though do not harass. Following up with an email shows that you are serious. If you make an appointment to meet someone, either for an initial visit or interview, be sure to show up on time. This shows respect for the person you would like to interview. If you know you will be late or need to cancel, communicate this as soon as possible. After the meeting or interview, always thank your narrators for the opportunity.

CONTACTING NARRATORS YOU ALREADY KNOW: If you are planning on conducting an interview with someone you already know (friend, family member, peer), follow the same basic procedures as the ones listed above. The formality of the process will enable both the interviewer and the narrator to focus on the details of that working relationship, which will facilitate a more authentic oral history experience.

LEARNING ABOUT YOUR NARRATOR

In order to be prepared for each interview, make sure students have conducted some research regarding their narrators. If there is no information available in print or online, students can ask their narrator to write a brief autobiographical sketch of themselves. This can be sent via email, text, or collected in person. Students may want to exchange autobiographical sketches with their narrators. If that is not possible or appropriate, it is essential that students ask their narrators, "Is there anything you would like to know about me?" Ultimately, this process will enable students to create informed interview questions.

While students are learning about their narrators, remind them to be open to, and mindful of, any cultural norms or differences they will need to consider before conducting their interviews. For instance, in some cultures, direct eye contact can be considered disrespectful. In other cultures, it may be the norm. This information may influence how students create their interview environment.

CRAFTING THE INTERVIEW

If we take time to listen, we'll find wisdom, wonder, and poetry in the lives and stories of the people all around us. —*Dave Isay, Founder and President, StoryCorps*

The next two sections of the guide focus on the heart of oral history: the interview. In this part, various practical elements of conducting interviews are covered, some of which may include steps in the process that may be obvious, and some of which may be more often overlooked. The focus is on the "art" of the interview—qualities that move beyond journalistic functions and into the special nature of practicing oral history.

CREATING ORAL HISTORY INTERVIEW QUESTIONS

Generating inclusive, open-ended interview questions lies at the center of the oral history experience. Creating questions that narrators can respond to with detailed, personal experiences not only makes for a successful interview, but also reflects the Voice of Witness oral history framework of honoring individuals. By crafting thoughtful, informed questions, students demonstrate an understanding of their narrators' background—an understanding that is communicated to the narrator as genuine interest in his or her story. The following activities and modeling exercises can give students valuable practice in shaping "story-generator" questions and learning how fluid interviews can be.

THE QUESTION GAME

TIME NEEDED: 20–25 minutes

MATERIALS: Black/white board, and notebooks.

OBJECTIVE: To help students understand the difference between "closed" and "open" questions, and which ones are appropriate for an oral history interview.

RELATED CORE CURRICULUM STANDARDS: Speaking and Listening SL.9–10.1, SL.11–12.1, SL.9–10.3, SL.11–12.3.

STEP ONE: Have students write down three questions they might like to ask you, the teacher. Draw a T chart on the board, with "class" listed above one side, and your name written above the other.

> Intro: *We're going to play a game today in which you can ask me questions, and I'll answer them (within reason). Now, I'm looking for certain types of questions. If you ask me the type of question I'm looking for, you get a point. If you don't, I get a point.*
>
> *I'm not going to tell you anymore about what I'm looking for in the questions. You will start to see what the "winning" questions have in common.*

STEP TWO: Call on different students, listening to and answering their questions. If they ask questions that require only a yes/no or factual answer, put a point in your column. If they ask a question that requires an opinion, some thoughtfulness, a description, etc., put a point in their column. It can be helpful to exaggerate this some, really going into a story with the first few open questions volunteered.

As the game progresses, students will probably continue to ask closed questions. As they do, ask their classmates what could be added to their questions so that the class gets a point. Usually they will start adding "why" and "how" and "could you explain" to their peers' questions.

STEP THREE: When they have won, stop and have students explain how you got points (what those questions had in common) and then how they got points (what those questions had in common). Write these ideas down on the board and have students recall how they changed some questions with a few words to give the class points.

STEP FOUR: Label the questions "open" and "closed." Tell students they want to ask mostly open questions in their interview so that their interviewee will tell stories, not just give facts. But also let them know that a few closed questions at the beginning (to get the interviewee comfortable and to get some basics, like name spellings and place of birth) can be really helpful.

STEP FIVE: Give students a few minutes to write a couple of open questions for the interview they are going to do. Do a check for understanding with pairs and with the whole class to make sure they understand.

STEP SIX: For homework, assign a full question-writing exercise for the students' interviews.

THE AUTOBIOGRAPHICAL SKETCH EXERCISE (20 minutes)

A good way to give students practice creating solid interview questions is for them to write short autobiographical sketches. The sketches do not have to be longer than a paragraph and should contain some personal history and interesting accomplishments or experiences. Remind students that it is their choice about what to include in their sketches, and tell them that they are going to be sharing their sketches with classmates.

SAMPLE STUDENT AUTOBIOGRAPHICAL SKETCH *(Courtesy of Mission San Jose High School, Fremont, CA)*

"I was born on February 5, 1996. My first Christmas was spent in the hospital for lung malformation, which I continued to have until I was two. I attended preschool and went to kindergarten at Mission Valley. My brother was born February 8, 2002. I finished K-6 at Mission Valley. I attended Hopkins for seventh and eighth grade. Currently, I attend Mission San Jose High School as a sophomore. I enjoy piano (which I've been playing since first grade), distance running, and watching movies."

After they have finished their sketches, students exchange them with a classmate and practice creating interview questions based on the information provided in the sketches.

SAMPLE AUTOBIOGRAPHICAL SKETCH INTERVIEW QUESTIONS:

- *What details can you tell me about your lung malformation?*
- *What memories do you have about kindergarten?*
- *Can you describe your relationship with your brother?*
- *Tell me about your most exhilarating experience as a pianist.*
- *What are the similarities between playing piano and distance running?*

This activity can be directly followed by a short practice interview and the longer practice interview listed on page 117.

MODELING AN INTERVIEW: THE "MYSTERY GUEST" INTERVIEW

TIME NEEDED: Two class periods (plus some preparation).

MATERIALS: "Mystery Guest" autobiographical sketches, paper, pen/pencil, and notebook.

OBJECTIVE: To practice interviewing skills and to formulate interview questions.

RELATED CORE CURRICULUM STANDARDS: Reading Literature RL.9-10.1, RL.9-10.2. Speaking and Listening L.9-10.1. Writing W.9-10.1.

OVERVIEW

In this exercise, students will have the opportunity to hone their ability to generate and ask interview questions. When conducting an interview, it is always difficult to ask the right questions, the questions that will prompt the interviewee to really open up, and tell an unexpected story, something more interesting than just standard biographical information. Learning to create these questions both before the interview and while the interviewee is talking takes practice. This exercise lets students practice these skills. In addition, students will feel a better connection and deeper understanding of their school administrators and vice versa.

PREPARATION

STEP ONE: Ask three of your school administrators to each write an autobiographical sketch. Tell them not to spend more than ten to fifteen minutes on their sketches. To honor their busy schedules, allow them at least four weeks to complete their "assignment."

STEP TWO: Once sketches are submitted, compile the stories onto one page, front and back. Label each administrator *Mystery Guest 1, 2, 3*, and so on.

STEP THREE: After you and your administrators have all agreed on a date for "Mystery Guest" interviews, the administrators can decide among themselves which classes/periods each will visit. The interviews should only last approximately fifteen to twenty minutes, so they should not need to worry about time constraints or being out of the office for too long. Fortunately, your classes will be prepared for each administrator, so it will not matter who shows up.

In the meantime, during one class period, have your students write their own autobiographical sketches in their notebooks. Again, allow them only ten to fifteen minutes to write their sketches. Have students work in pairs and practice creating questions based on each other's sketches. If there is time, they may even interview one another.

STEP ONE: Read the Mystery Guests' sketches aloud.

STEP TWO: After each sketch, have students develop five questions for each guest. Encourage them to create questions that can "fill in the gaps" of the guest's sketch.

STEP THREE: Give each student an index card. Have students write their favorite question for each guest on card. *Alternative:* Have students work in small groups to develop questions for each Mystery Guest.

STEP FOUR: Read submitted questions and select which ones you feel will be most effective for the Mystery Guest interviews. *Alternative:* You and the students can choose the most effective questions together.

STEP FIVE (optional): It can be helpful to model interviews with students so that they can get a feel for what the process is like. To practice, have students write questions for each other and interview in pairs. Get some feedback from them about what made them most comfortable, what made them want to talk a lot and tell stories, etc. Then have a few students interview each other in front of the class. Interrupt them occasionally to have the class analyze the interviewer's use of open questions, the order of questions, etc.

DAY TWO

STEP ONE: Before the interviews begin, tell students to take out their notebooks. The notebooks are not for writing down their Mystery Guest's answers. Instead, students are to write down additional questions they may have for their guest as the interview takes place.

STEP TWO: An administrator arrives for each period. Have your guest sit in front of the class and ask them selected questions. *Alternative:* Students ask administrator selected questions. If there is time, students may ask their additional questions.

STEP THREE: Thank the administrator for coming. You may want to consider having your students write thank-you notes to their guest.

ADDITIONAL STRATEGIES FOR CRAFTING INTERVIEW QUESTIONS

THREE LEVELS OF INQUIRY

Encourage students to let their interviews evolve organically by mixing specific questions with more general ones. Some teachers have guided their students toward creating interview questions with three levels of inquiry.

Level one questions are more general, such as "Where did you grow up?" or "What was your favorite subject in school?"

Level two questions become more specific, but also more open-ended. Questions such as "What do you do to prepare for a math test?" Or "Describe what it feels like to ace a math test."

Level three questions narrow the focus to a particular instance or event: "Tell me the story of the day you were accused of cheating on a math test." This approach can help students develop "flow" during their interviews and respond to their narrators in a more natural way. It can also steer students away from asking "yes" or "no" questions.

FOLLOW-UP QUESTIONS

Sometimes the most powerful questions students can ask during an interview are the ones they did not prepare in advance. As students are listening to their narrator during the course of the interview, they may hear something they would really like to go back to or hear more about. Not only will their narrator appreciate hearing details of their story reflected back to them, but this also creates an opportunity for students to "go deeper" with their questions. For example:

> *"You had mentioned your experiences with _____ a few minutes ago. Could you describe the details of that experience?"*

Being in the moment and letting follow-up questions occur to students during the interview can enrich and enliven the experience for both parties.

COMMUNICATION SKILLS AND CONDUCTING THE INTERVIEW

"I feel that attentive listening is by far the most important skill in conducting oral histories, and it doesn't necessarily come naturally to most of us. It's very easy to get ahead of your narrator and to lose attention as you get ready to ask new questions or shift focus...In normal conversations we are accustomed to breaking in with our own opinions and experiences, but in the course of an oral history I've found that I need to stay completely focused on my interviewee, to stay on the same wavelength and be ready to follow-up at every turn. That requires some serious listening skills."
—Joell Hallowell, Voice of Witness Interviewer, *Underground America*

Many of the skills required for a successful oral history interview have been covered in the previous section. This section focuses on communication skills necessary for an "authentic" oral history experience and ultimately will allow both student interviewer and narrator to "be in the moment" and find connection. This section will also discuss the details of creating an ideal environment for the interview to take place, and provide activities and handouts for practice interviews.

COMMUNICATION SKILLS

Addressing the communication skills required for an oral history interview is a good place to begin when preparing students for their interviews. It can be intimidating for students to think of it in these technical terms, so you can frame it in a way that reminds them of something they already know. At Voice of Witness, we have framed this in the form of a question:

> *"If you needed to have an important discussion with a friend or family member, what would you need from them in order to feel safe sharing?"*

COMMUNICATION BRAINSTORM

TIME NEEDED: 10–12 minutes

MATERIALS: Paper, pens, pencils and/or whiteboard and markers.

OBJECTIVE: Create opportunities for students to connect personal experience with essential oral history interview skills.

RELATED CORE CURRICULUM STANDARDS: Speaking and Listening SL.9–10.1, SL.11–12.1.

STEP ONE: Write the following question on the classroom whiteboard or in students' journals or notebooks (feel free to adapt the question to suit your students):

"If you need to discuss an important matter with a friend or family member, what would you need from them in order to feel safe sharing?"

STEP TWO: Students call out or write down their responses to the question. Make sure they write down everyone's response. Encourage them to be specific, with prompts like:

- How can you show or communicate that during a conversation?
- Can you give an example?

SAMPLE SKILLS:

- Trust
- Respect
- Listening
- Genuine interest
- Understanding
- Eye contact
- Attentive body language

STEP THREE: After sharing, remind students that the communication skills they have been discussing are not only essential skills to practice in preparation for their interviews, but also valuable life skills.

STEP FOUR: Provide the following handout for students, which can be used in conjunction with any practice interviews or read and filled out as homework.

Students should keep a copy of these guidelines in their project binders.

"THE FINE ART OF MAKING THE OTHER PERSON LOOK GOOD"

Here are a few pointers that will help you prepare for your oral history interview. Practice them with friends and family.

1. **GIVE YOUR NARRATOR YOUR UNDIVIDED ATTENTION.**

   Genuine interest and active listening are essential to a successful interview. Your narrator will appreciate the effort!

2. **DO NOT INTERRUPT YOUR NARRATOR BECAUSE YOU HAVE THOUGHT OF A GREAT QUESTION.**

   If your narrator is in the middle of a story or finishing a thought, do not interrupt. You will probably be able to ask that great question as a follow-up sometime during the interview.

3. **DO NOT LET PERIODS OF SILENCE FLUSTER YOU.**

   Sometimes we become uncomfortable with silence and leap into those silences with a comment or question. Silences during an interview can be useful as your narrator is thinking about something or is considering sharing a particular story.

4. **AN INTERVIEW IS NOT A DIALOGUE.**

   The main goal when conducting an oral history interview is to let your narrator do most of the talking! Sometimes during an interview, your narrator will be sharing a story that reminds you of something similar in your own life. You will naturally want to share your story. In that moment, make a "silent connection" with your narrator. It will increase the empathy between you and your narrator will appreciate the quality of your attention.

5. **STAY OPEN AND BE YOURSELF.**

   Oral history interviews can go in directions that you cannot always anticipate. That is part of the fun! Go with the flow and stay open to what is happening in the moment. Expressing your personality and sense of humor during the interview will inspire your narrator to express his or hers.

THE PRACTICE INTERVIEW

TIME NEEDED: One class period.

MATERIALS: Pens, paper, pencils, interview questions from the Autobiographical Sketch activity (p. 98), and digital voice recorder (optional).

OBJECTIVE: Develop speech and communication skills through the oral history interview process.

RELATED CORE CURRICULUM STANDARDS: Speaking and Listening SL.9–10.1, SL.11–12.1, SL.9–10.4, SL.11–12.4.

OVERVIEW

While students may have had opportunities for short practice interviews during earlier "modeling" activities, the following practice interview activity will enable students to really "dig in" and hone their skills during a longer interview session.

STEP ONE: Students should pair up with their partners from the Autobiographical Sketch activity. Allow each student to add or rewrite any interview questions. Remind students about **the three levels of inquiry** and **follow-up questions** (5–7 minutes).

STEP TWO: Depending on classroom space, have students either spread out in the room or have pairs work in different rooms (if the pairs are too close to each other, they can get "pulled in" to another pair's interview). Each pair then decides who will be interviewed first (5 minutes).

STEP THREE: Before starting their practice interviews have interviewers introduce themselves and their narrators (1 minute).

SAMPLE INTRO: "This is an interview with (narrator name), conducted by (interviewer's name) on (today's date, month, and year)."

STEP FOUR: Each pair then begins their practice interview. After fifteen minutes, interviewer and narrator switch and the next practice interview begins. Interviews can be shorter for younger students if desired. During practice interviews, let pairs know when they have five and then two minutes left (20–30 minutes).

STEP FIVE: Class comes together for a short "debrief" from their practice interviews. Among other responses, some questions to consider (10 minutes):

- What did you find challenging?
- What did you learn about yourself during the practice interview?

- What will you take away from this practice that you would like to incorporate during your project interview?

STEP SIX (optional): An additional practice interview can be done as homework, following the guidelines of the Autobiographical Sketch activity.

INTERVIEW LOGISTICS: RECORDING AND LOCATION

RECORDING YOUR INTERVIEW

There are many ways in which to record an oral history interview. The methods and devices used will depend on individual projects, budgets, and curricular goals. Voice of Witness uses digital audio recorders that have USB ports for easy downloading onto a computer to make transcribing and editing easier. Many other devices can be used to create MP3s (for Mac) or Windows Media Files (for PCs): iPhones, iPads, and many cell phones have the capacity for voice recording and downloading. Flip cameras and other video equipment can be used for recording interviews as well—especially if students desire a strong visual component in their projects. Whatever recording device chosen, students should make sure there is sufficient memory and the capacity to save the recorded interview.

THE RIGHT LOCATION FOR YOUR INTERVIEW

First and foremost, students should conduct their interviews in a quiet space, with a minimum of street sounds, other voices, or the rattling of air circulation devices. A small table comes in handy for taking notes and for placing digital recorders. A room that has natural light or forgiving ambient light is preferable—glaring fluorescent light can easily make interviews feel like interrogations. A quiet café is a good option.

Older students can consider going to a narrator's home or place of business. Depending on students' ages, time constraints, and other practicalities, all interviews may need to be conducted on campus with adult supervision if necessary. Regardless of location, the goal is to find and create an environment where a narrator is comfortable enough to speak freely.

ONCE THE INTERVIEW IS COMPLETED

"Imagining what it is like to be someone other than oneself is at the core of our humanity. It is the essence of compassion, and it is the beginning of morality." —*Ian McEwan*

THANK-YOU NOTES

After you have finished your interview, make sure you follow up with your narrator to thank them. People's time is precious and interviews can be taxing and time-consuming. Thank-you letters, emails, and phone calls are all appropriate. Make your narrator feel appreciated. That is the point after all!

STORING AND SAVING YOUR RECORDED INTERVIEW

Make sure to save and back up your recorded interviews on a portable hard drive and take care not to erase them! You will need to refer to them for corrections and fact-checking. The raw, unedited recordings form an important archive and should be maintained as a courtesy to your narrator as well as a matter of keeping a "public record" of your interview.

LISTENING AND EAR TRAINING

The first class meeting after students have conducted their interviews can be very enjoyable. There is usually a mixture of excitement and relief as they are eager to share their experiences. It is a good idea to begin by acknowledging their courage and professionalism. Many of them have come far out of their comfort zones! Allow time for students to share the challenges and rewards of the interview experience.

During this "debrief," students should play back short portions of their interview for the entire class to hear. It provides practice listening for the sections of the interview that sound compelling and energized—moments when narrators felt unself-conscious and were able speak freely about their experiences. This "ear training" will help students make strong choices as they begin to transcribe and edit their interviews.

LISTENING TO THE ENTIRE INTERVIEW

The next step is for students to listen to their interviews in their entirety. If students conduct (on average) thirty-minute interviews, then it should take about forty-five minutes to listen to each one. What adds the extra fifteen minutes? It is time that students will use to take notes on which parts of the interview are authentic. Students should also note the times of these sections, so they can easily return to them during the transcription process.

FOLLOW-UP INTERVIEW QUESTIONS

After listening to their interviews and taking notes, students (with guidance from the teacher) should consider the following questions:

- Was there a missed opportunity during the interview?
- Would the interview feel incomplete without asking some follow-up questions?
- Has the interview satisfied the goals of the project?
- By listening to the interview, have I given thought to the pivotal moments within the larger story?

PART 4

SHAPING ORAL HISTORY NARRATIVES

"It's amazing how dramatic facts can be." —*Elia Kazan*

OVERVIEW

Editing oral history is where commitment to accuracy in retelling someone else's story and creating a readable, compelling narrative becomes technical. It is the most time-consuming part of the process because it includes transcribing—but shaping an oral history can also be the most rewarding. This section will provide the resources to guide students through the written process of editing oral history. It may be helpful to think of the task in terms of three steps: transcribing, editing, and proofing.

The transcribing phase of the oral history process is challenging on many levels. It helps to be explicit with students about the value of attending to this phase arduously. While they have probably heard expressions like "every word counts," now they have a chance to see firsthand how important it is to "weigh words." We also offer a few suggestions for bringing this part of the assignment down to a manageable period of time.

Two editors from the Voice of Witness book series offer the following comments about the biggest challenges of editing oral history:

"At the editing stage, making decisions about what's at the heart of the story—and having to make difficult edits/cuts that are interesting in themselves but which don't serve the story as a whole." —*mimi lok, Executive Director,* Voice of Witness

"I think to do a very effective oral history you have to respect the story the person is telling you. And that means realizing they probably haven't spoken about this publicly, and this is the first time someone has asked them to tell their story." —*Sandra Hernandez, Interviewer,* Underground America

TIPS AND ADVICE FOR TRANSCRIBING AN INTERVIEW

There is no getting around it: transcribing is a time-consuming process. Make sure you give yourself plenty of time to write out everything you need. A general rule of thumb: it usually takes about four to five hours to transcribe an hour of audio.

PREPARATION

Find a quiet place to work with your recorder or computer (if you have downloaded your interview), earphones, and/or notepad.

TRANSCRIPTION METHODS

There is no standard method for transcription. Some people press play, listen to six words, press pause, write down the words, and repeat. Others will listen to the whole tape, taking as many words as they can, and then return to the beginning and go through more slowly, filling out their initial notes. In both approaches, *make sure you record the time-code periodically* (every few minutes) so that you have an easy reference point later between the hard copy transcript and the audio files.

Your transcript should include the interviewer's questions, even though you will probably edit them out later. If you want, you can note other aspects of the interview in brackets within the text. For example, if the interviewee begins to cry at some point, it might be prudent to include {begins crying} in the transcription. Later, when you edit, you can decide if this should be part of the narrative.

ACCURACY

The foremost concern when transcribing an interview is accuracy. This means that you will have to listen to some sections a few times to get them right. It is important to keep the speaker's word usage, syntax, and idiosyncrasies intact. It is also important that you watch your grammar, so that the sentence maintains its original meaning. Some examples:

IF THE SPEAKER SAYS:

I ran from house to house—everyone's house, even Ray's. Couldn't find a cornbread recipe.

YOU MIGHT BE TEMPTED TO TYPE:

I ran from house to house—everybody's house, even Ray's. Couldn't find a cornbread recipe.

OR:

I ran from house to house, everyone's house, even Ray's, couldn't find a cornbread recipe.

If you hear "everyone," don't type "everybody." If you are not sure what you are hearing, rewind and check it again. If you are not sure about how to punctuate a sentence, use periods to separate thoughts. Even if it is incorrect, readers will get the idea.

SAMPLE ORAL HISTORY TRANSCRIPT

TYPING YOUR TRANSCRIPT

Transcripts follow a strict format:

- Single-spaced, typed
- 12-point font, Times or Times New Roman
- Names of interviewer and interviewee written out and in bold for first question and response
- Initials of interviewer and interviewee only in bold for additional responses
- Only internal dialogue or thoughts in quotation marks
- Include all laughs, coughs, etc.

EXAMPLE

Lisa Morehouse: What memories do you have of Vietnam?

Viet Nguyen: Umm, *(coughs)* I don't have many clear memories of Vietnam, mostly of school.

LM: What do you remember about school?

VN: Well, before the, my dad had been working against the Communists before the war, they had a house, land, and so after the war I went to a Communist school, learned speeches and stuff, so that it appeared that our family was compliant, going along, and I remember thinking, "Why do I have to wear this uniform, learn these songs?"

SELECTIVE TRANSCRIBING

The selective transcribing process allows students to hone their narrative and ear-training skills by just transcribing sections of the interview that feel compelling, energized, conflicted, or otherwise interesting. It can also keep the time spent on this phase of the process to a manageable length. Keep in mind that this process can be problematic if used too liberally, but very helpful if used wisely.

Students have a knack for knowing a good story when they hear one. They have a solid grasp of the elements of storytelling: humor, suspense, emotion, juxtaposition, and conflict. Find ways to honor their skills in this area. Allow students to get second opinions from teachers, parents, and peers.

Have students identify one or more passages of the interview, say ten minutes from a thirty-minute interview, that really capture the essence of the speaker's story and simply transcribe that section. Just make sure there are not other places that could be integrated to this passage that have been overlooked. When in doubt, more is better! Students can always cut it out later, but it is much harder and more time consuming going back through audio files to find passages you thought you would not need.

EDITING

This section will be devoted to the skills and choices of editing an oral history narrative, providing students with strategies and guidelines. Oral history stories are different from fiction or even nonfiction, but they are still stories. As an editor, the goal is to help the narrator tell his or her story in the best possible way. Editing is both an objective exercise (grammatical rules must be observed) and a subjective one (the order of the narrative is the editor's choice). Ultimately, this is about telling a good story. But editors do not actually tell the story, they *facilitate* it. Editing takes practice so do not be afraid to try different things!

PROCEDURES FOR EDITING
ORAL HISTORY NARRATIVES

EDITING BASICS

1. Remember the basics of creating a good story: chronology, style, interesting characters, exciting events, and emotion.
2. Make sure that the narrator's "voice" is never lost or compromised! (Remember your goal of honoring them.)
3. Edit your transcript so the narrative has a clear beginning, middle, and end. Reorder the chronology of the narrator's recollection if necessary.
4. Take out the interviewer's questions and comments.
5. Clean up typos, break up run-on sentences, change tenses for consistency, and cut words and phrases that do not fit. You will have to make some important decisions about how "polished" you are going to make the narrative. (Keep in mind consideration #1.)
6. Try to strike a balance between preserving the voice of the narrator and correcting any grammatical errors that will distract from the telling of the story.
7. Do your best to reflect the narrator's intelligence—for example, lack of fluency in English (or any other language) certainly does not reflect a lack of fluency in the narrator's thought process.
8. Occasionally, you may find that portions of your transcript do not make sense without some information from your interview question. You can add some words from your questions to make your interviewee's answers clear, as long as you add these words in brackets [ ].

Here's an example:

RB: Where did you originally come from?
TP: Lake Providence, Louisiana.

For this to make sense without the question, you would have to add some words like:

{I came from} Lake Providence, Louisiana.

You can also add *conjunctions* (and, but, or) and *articles* (the, an, a) if they make the story clearer.

9. Since you are facilitating someone else's story and cannot add characters or exciting events, what *can* you do?

- Aim to make the person's story clearer
- Aim to bring out their personality, their style
- Aim to make sure those elements of a good story are included

EDITING PRACTICE SHEET

SAMPLE TRANSCRIPT TO EDIT AS A CLASS

My name is John Knight and I was born in Concord Massachusetts on February 24, 1987. I grew up on a small farm in New Hampshire where we had chickens and cats and dogs and horses. My mother loved riding and she always tried to get my sister and me to ride with her but I never really liked it. It was always such a bumpy ride that my butt hurt afterward and I was afraid I'd get thrown off like I saw people get thrown off in olden western movies.

My sister liked it though, she's a very good rider. My sister is three years younger than I am and she lives in Colorado now. It's where she goes to school. College. Her name is Becca. Even though I don't see her very often because we live in different places, she is still a good friend of mine and we talk together a lot on the phone. She calls for advice and stuff and I usually call just to tell her what I've been thinking about. I miss her sometimes, but I'm glad we have those experiences we do.

When we were kids, my sister and I had to entertain ourselves because there wasn't much to do on the farm. We used to go swimming and build hay-forts in our barn. We used to spend a lot of time down at our pond, catching frogs. Well, I would catch frogs and she would make sure they didn't get out of the bucket. She didn't like to touch them, afraid they'd give her warts. She's like that—always afraid of germs and things. Occasionally we'd find frog eggs and put them in a bucket up by the house, hoping that we'd see them hatch and turn from eggs to tadpoles to frogs.

SOME THINGS TO LOOK OUT FOR:

- Run-on sentences—break them up and add punctuation
- Order—make sure the narrative does not jump around too much. For instance, you might want to switch the last two paragraphs in the above example to maintain fluidity.
- Get rid of excessive words like "ums" and unnecessary repetition

SAMPLE EDITED NARRATIVE:

My name is John Knight and I was born in Concord Massachusetts on February 24, 1987. I grew up on a small farm in New Hampshire where we had chickens, cats, dogs, and horses. My mother loved riding and she always tried to get my sister and me to ride with her. But I never really liked it. It was always such a bumpy ride that my butt hurt afterward and I was afraid I'd get thrown off. My sister liked it though. She's a very good rider.

When we were kids, my sister and I had to entertain ourselves because there wasn't much to do on the farm. We used to go swimming and build hay-forts in our barn. We used to spend a lot of time down at our pond, catching frogs. Well, I would catch frogs and she would make sure they didn't get out of the bucket. She didn't like to touch them because she thought they'd give her warts. She's like that—always afraid of germs. Occasionally, we'd find frog eggs and put them in a bucket up by the house, hoping that we'd see them hatch.

My sister is three years younger than me and she lives in Colorado where she goes to college. Her name is Becca. Even though I don't see her very often, she is still a good friend of mine and we talk together often on the phone. She calls for advice and I usually call just to tell her what I've been thinking. I miss her sometimes, but I'm glad we have the experiences we do together.

PROOFREADING

When students are finished editing (a process that may take several passes to get it right), it is important to encourage them to proofread their work. Very often this step is taken lightly and narratives are then published with mistakes. Not only does this reflect poorly on the student, but also on the person whose story has been told. If one of the goals is to honor a person, it is crucial to do everything possible to portray them articulately and well.

SHARING WITH YOUR NARRATOR

Whenever possible, edited versions of Voice of Witness narratives are sent to narrators for their review and approval. This practice is consistent with our framework of honoring individuals and wanting to present their stories in an accurate, respectful way. Teachers should consider incorporating this practice and adding it to the student oral history checklist.

PART 5

AMPLIFYING ORAL HISTORIES

"What is one of the greatest rewards of oral history? When you feel you've captured someone's story and voice accurately when a narrator looks at the final draft and says, Yes, that's how it happened, that's how I told it. Also when the story's been shaped in a way that engages and moves readers."
—*mimi lok, Executive Director/Editor, Voice of Witness*

OVERVIEW

In many ways, a successful oral history project can end after the student submits the final draft of the edited and polished narrative. A great follow up is to have students read their narratives to each other. But to truly honor the people who have told their stories, it is important to share their narratives in a broader context. Oral history is often most powerful when a voice can be perpetuated. These are important stories, after all, and they make no difference unless we share them.

An evening of dramatic readings can be a great "amplification" of your oral history project. Some teachers use the narratives as a springboard for other public performances: poetry, drama, dance, and music. Many students are eager to put their narratives online.

As your students are creating their oral history projects, encourage them to be thinking about how they plan to share their stories from the beginning. This decision might change the way a project is carried out. For instance a project that will eventually be part of a website might include more audio and video, which a narrative art piece wouldn't. If you are going to do a community sharing, how can you make an engaging presentation from oral history transcripts?

DELIVERY SYSTEMS
Ways to Feature the Narrative

ONLINE

The most common ways to share oral histories is online. Encourage your students to create websites using interfaces like Wordpress, Weebly, Tumblr, or Google Sites. These are simple, easy-to-use, and free website design services where students can post video, audio, images, and text. Have students use Facebook and other social networking sites to encourage their friends and family to visit their sites. Transom and Soundcloud are particularly useful for learning how to download and share audio.

PUBLISH A BOOK/PHOTO ESSAYS

Self-publishing has become increasingly easy these days and relatively inexpensive. Services like Lulu, Createspace, and Lightning Source are great places to start.

They Don't Understand: A Photo Essay Book
(Courtesy of Nancy T. and Mayra R., Envision Academy of Arts and Technology, Oakland, CA)

VIDEO

Examples of video work from a pilot project by Voice of Witness and Facing History and Ourselves can be viewed on the Facing History and Ourselves website: *www.facinghistory.org/about/who/profiles/voice-witness-students-build-di*

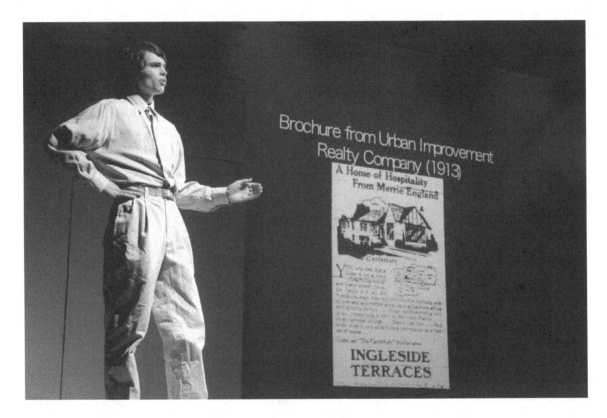

LIVE PERFORMANCE

The following is a sample "script" from *The OMI Project*, created by students at Lick-Wilmerding High School in San Francisco about the history of the neighborhood surrounding the school.

The OMI Project: Oral History Theatrical Performance
(photo courtesy of Robert Sanborn)

Woody LaBounty: The houses were supposed to be a certain price and they had to have a certain amount of lawn around them. They wanted no businesses in there, no chicken farms, no anything. It had to be a high-class residential park. Another thing about this residential park: no minorities. Minorities couldn't buy. They couldn't rent. They could only be there as servants for the people that owned it. This was the whole idea to make it exclusive. So not only do you not have to worry about having a chicken farm or a grocery store next to your house, don't worry. There won't be any people of color to bother you either.

Margie Whitnah: My mother's Mexican, born in Mexico and moved here when she was young to Ocean Ave. and lived a little bit in Mission Beach with her sister—five sisters and one brother in the family. "You sit in the back of the streetcar, I'm going to be in the front, because it looks bad to have that many children now in the United States. She'd do things that were kind of unusual like powder their faces to make them look more Anglo and put long socks on my mom so her hairy legs wouldn't show. Things like that. She was trying to fit in and the kids had this double message.

NARRATIVE PAINTING

Taking the oral history narrative as inspiration, have students represent their narrator through an original and creative visual art piece. Students can use their encounters and interviews, along with photographs as the foundation for the art piece. Using technical skills and creative approaches, students can generate high-quality pieces of art using a variety of materials and filled with visual metaphors.

Encourage students to think about who, what, and where their subject has come from.

This can be done in two parts, including 1) a Narrative Art Piece in which students represent someone's identity and "story" in a dynamic art piece layered with portraiture, metaphor, and symbolism, and 2) the Artist Statement. This is a typed statement that complements the art piece and explains its reasoning in great detail.

Narrative Painting: *Untitled*
(Courtesy of Laneisha B., Envision Academy, Oakland, CA)

Oral History Comic Book, *The Mentor*
(*courtesy of F. Chen, D. Vo, C. Mai, and S. Shi of Mission San Jose High School, Fremont, CA*)

PART 6

EDUCATOR RESOURCES: CURRICULAR STANDARDS AND TEACHING STRATEGIES FOR ORAL HISTORY

CURRICULUM STANDARDS FOR ORAL HISTORY

While it is not the aim of Voice of Witness to provide the means of "teaching to the test," we aim to provide teachers with materials and pedagogy that are engaging, historically relevant, intellectually challenging, and civic minded. Rather than teaching to the test, we are teaching to the skills. Nonetheless, we realize that there are standards and guidelines that teachers must follow. The following lists the standards from the Common Core Standards that our curriculum satisfies.

READING HISTORY

KEY IDEAS AND DETAIL

- RH.9–10.1. Cite specific textual evidence to support analysis of primary and secondary sources, attending to such features as the date and origin of the information.
- RH.9–10.2. Determine the central ideas or information of a primary or secondary source; provide an accurate summary of how key events or ideas develop over the course of the text.
- RH.9–10.3. Analyze in detail a series of events described in a text; determine whether earlier events caused later ones or simply preceded them.

CRAFT AND STRUCTURE

- RH.9–10.4. Determine the meaning of words and phrases as they are used in a text, including vocabulary describing political, social, or economic aspects of history/social science.
- RH.9–10.5. Analyze how a text uses structure to emphasize key points or advance an explanation or analysis.
- RH.9–10.6. Compare the point of view of two or more authors for how they treat the same or similar topics, including which details they include and emphasize in their respective accounts.

INTEGRATION OF KNOWLEDGE AND IDEAS

- RH.9–10.7. Integrate quantitative or technical analysis (e.g., charts, research data) with qualitative analysis in print or digital text.
- RH.9–10.8. Assess the extent to which the reasoning and evidence in a text support the author's claims.
- RH.9–10.9. Compare and contrast treatments of the same topic in several primary and secondary sources.

RANGE OF READING AND LEVEL OF TEXT COMPLEXITY

- RH.9–10.10. By the end of grade 10, read and comprehend history/social studies texts in the grades 9–10 text complexity band independently and proficiently.

SPEAKING AND LISTENING

COMPREHENSION AND COLLABORATION

- SL.9–10.1. Initiate and participate effectively in a range of collaborative discussions (one-on-one, in groups, and teacher-led) with diverse partners on grades 9–10 topics, texts, and issues, building on others' ideas and expressing their own clearly and persuasively.
- SL.9–10.2. Integrate multiple sources of information presented in diverse media or formats (e.g., visually, quantitatively, orally), evaluating the credibility and accuracy of each source.
- SL.-9–10.3. Evaluate a speaker's point of view, reasoning, and use of evidence and rhetoric, identifying any fallacious reasoning or exaggerated or distorted evidence.

PRESENTATION OF KNOWLEDGE AND IDEAS

- SL.9–10.5. Make strategic use of digital media (e.g., textual, graphical, audio, visual, and interactive elements) in presentations to enhance understanding of findings, reasoning, and evidence and to add interest.

WRITING

TEXT TYPES AND PURPOSES

- W.910.1. Write arguments to support claims in an analysis of substantive topics or texts, using valid reasoning and relevant and sufficient evidence.
- W.9–10.2. Write informative/explanatory texts to examine and convey complex ideas, concepts, and information clearly and accurately through the effective selection, organization, and analysis of content.
- W.9–10.3. Write narratives to develop real or imagined experiences or events using effective technique, well-chosen details, and well-structured event sequences.

PRODUCTION AND DISTRIBUTION OF WRITING

- W.9–10.5. Develop and strengthen writing as needed by planning, revising, editing, rewriting, or trying a new approach, focusing on addressing what is most significant for a specific purpose and audience.

"These standards emphasize historical narrative, highlight the roles of significant individuals throughout history, and convey the rights and obligations of citizenship." —*History-Social Science Content Standards for California Public Schools*

"Through literature, moreover, students experience the unique history of the United States in an immediate way and encounter many cultures that exist both within and beyond this nation's borders." —*English Content Standards for California Public Schools*

ORAL HISTORY SKILL SETS AND LEARNING OUTCOMES

In the course of an oral history project, students have an opportunity to develop academic and arts-based skills in the following areas (which can vary given the scope of individual projects):

HISTORY/SOCIAL SCIENCES

- Critical historical analysis and research
- Community-based history and research
- Observable data analysis
- Learning civics through history
- Discovering political science and government

LANGUAGE/LITERACY AND COMMUNICATION

- Empathic listening
- Public speaking/oral communication
- Creative collaboration
- Interview techniques
- Transcription
- Vocabulary building
- Editing and shaping literary narratives
- The basic tenants of journalism and reporting

CIVIC ENGAGEMENT/BUILDING COMMUNITY

- Choosing to participate
- Building community partnerships
- Service learning/immersion
- Team building
- Cultivating cultural awareness and global citizenship

MEDIA/TECHNOLOGY

- Media literacy in sharing projects
- Video production
- Podcasts/internet radio production
- Media software
- Digital storytelling
- Website creation

VISUAL/PERFORMING/LITERARY ARTS

- Photography
- Drawing/painting
- Graphic novels
- Book making/publishing
- Performance: theater, music, dance

CRITICAL THINKING

- Understanding ascribed and personal identity
- Understanding the creation of "the other"
- Ethical reflection
- Cultivating self-awareness

TEACHING STRATEGIES

CONTRACTING

Reading and discussing oral history can bring up challenging and complicated emotions, concepts, and issues for students. Before engaging any of the Voice of Witness narratives in class, teachers may find it useful to use the following framework for creating a safe, respectful environment for all participants, courtesy of Facing History and Ourselves.

A classroom that explores oral history and issues of social justice must be a place where explicit rules and implicit norms protect everyone's right to speak; where differing perspectives can be heard and valued; where members take responsibility for themselves, each other, and the group as a whole; and where each member has a stake and a voice in collective decisions. Facing History calls these spaces reflective classroom communities. Reflective classroom communities often do not happen by accident; rather, they are deliberatively nurtured by students and teachers who have shared expectations about how classroom members will treat one another.

One way to help classroom communities establish shared norms is to discuss them openly in a process called "contracting." Sometimes this involves drafting and agreeing to a formal contract of behavior as well. The following are some tips for facilitating conversations and activities about contracting.

STEP ONE: Define the word *contract*. A contract implies that all parties have a responsibility in upholding the agreement, and an individual stake in the collective. Students can think about what it means for a classroom to have a contract.

STEP TWO: To prepare students to develop a class contract, ask them to reflect on their experiences as students in a classroom community. You might use a prompt to structure students' reflection:

- Give an example of a time either inside or outside the classroom when you have felt comfortable sharing your ideas or questions. What were the circumstances? What made you feel comfortable?
- Identify when you have felt comfortable sharing your ideas and questions in the classroom. What happened in those moments to help you feel comfortable?
- Identify when you have had ideas or questions but have not shared them. Why not? What was happening at those moments?

STEP THREE: Useful class contracts typically include several clearly defined rules or expectations, as well as consequences for those who do not fulfill their obligations as members of the classroom community. There are many ways to proceed with developing a classroom contract. For example, you can ask small groups of students to work together to write rules or "expectations" for the classroom community. We suggest keeping the list brief (e.g., three to five items) so that the norms can be easily remembered. As groups present, you can organize their ideas by theme. If there are any tensions or contradictions in the expectations that have been suggested, you can discuss them as a class. While the process includes students' ideas, ultimately it is the teacher's responsibility to ensure that the final contract will nurture a safe learning environment.

You can also share with students a list of norms, rules, or expectations that have been used in other classrooms. Ask students to discuss what they think about these norms. Which ones do they think would help the group create a safe, respectful, productive learning environment? Invite students to edit this list by deleting, revising, or adding to it. Here is a list of norms that have been used in previous Facing History classrooms:

- Listen with respect. Try to understand what someone is saying before rushing to judgment.
- Make comments using "I" statements.
- If you do not feel safe making a comment or asking a question, write the thought in your journal. You can share the idea with your teacher first and together come up with a safe way to share it with the rest of the class.
- If someone expresses an idea or question that helps your own learning, say "thank you."
- If someone says something that hurts or offends you, do not attack the person.
- Acknowledge that the comment—not the person—hurt your feelings and explain why.
- Put-downs are never okay.
- If you do not understand something, ask a question.
- Think with your head and your heart.
- Share the talking time—provide room for others to speak.
- Do not interrupt others while they are speaking.
- Write thoughts in your journal if you do not have time to say them during class.
- Journal responses do not have to be shared publicly.

Another way to help students develop a classroom contract is to have them envision what they would like to have happen during certain scenarios. Scenarios could be drawn from students' own experiences. They might include situations such as:

- When we have an idea or question we would like to share, we can…
- When we have an idea, but do not feel comfortable sharing it out loud, we can…
- When someone says something that we appreciate, we can…
- When someone says something that might be confusing or offensive, we can…
- To make sure all students have the opportunity to participate in a class discussion, we can…
- If we read or watch something that makes us feel sad or angry, we can…
- To show respect for the ideas of others, we can…

STEP FOUR: To initiate the classroom contract, you can have students participate in a celebratory signing ceremony. Students can sign their own copies or a large copy that is posted in the room. You might allow for brief remarks from students about how they think the contract will help provide a safe, productive learning community.

ACTIVE READING STRATEGIES

The following active reading strategies can be applied to any narrative in the Voice of Witness series and are designed to help students better understand what they are reading and become actively engaged with a story. Another active reading strategy (Talk to the Text) can be found on page 23.

ACTIVE READING STRATEGIES

SUMMARIZING While reading and at the end of sections or chapters of the story, restate the important information that has happened. A good summary answers the *who, what, where, when, why,* and *how* questions.

MAKING CONNECTIONS Based on the material and what is happening in the text, do you have any personal experiences that are similar to the story, the situation, or the characters? Is it like a story you have heard, a movie you have seen, a book you have read?

ASKING QUESTIONS While you are reading, periodically stop to ask questions about why characters are doing what they are doing, what certain things mean, and how elements within the story compare to each other.

MAKING PREDICTIONS Stop periodically and make guesses about what you think will happen next in the story and why.

CLARIFYING What is confusing? Restate what has just happened in a text. Answer questions you have previously recorded.

EVALUATING Evaluate the text, the characters, and what is happening in the story. Why do the characters act the way they do? Do you understand their actions?

VISUALIZING As you read, picture the images the author creates. Make a movie inside your head based on the author's words in the text.

DIALECTICAL READING JOURNAL

INTRODUCTION TO DIALECTICAL READING JOURNALS

Think of your dialectical reading journal as a dialogue with the text in which you ask questions and then find answers to them through closely examining and studying the text.

The journal consists of two major columns. On the left-hand side summarize details or include quotes from the text that you find interesting, important, challenging, surprising, or worth thinking about further (include the text page number as well). You need to put each passage into one of three categories on the left-hand side of the journal. These categories consist of three symbols: **R, !, and ?**

R ROW: In the left-hand side of the R row write down a passage or quote from the text that reminds you of something. On the right-hand side of the R row explain what the passage reminds you of and how this helps you better understand the text.

! ROW: In the left-hand side of the ! row write down a passage or quote from the text that surprised you. On the right-hand side of the ! row explain how and why this passage surprised you and what you now better understand about the text.

? ROW: In the left-hand side of the ? row write down a passage or quote from the text that you have a question about. On the right-hand side of the ? row explain how you can attempt to answer this question and how it will better help you understand the text. Answering these questions will help you better understand the text.

EXPECTATIONS

Your journal will be most effective if you stop periodically as you are reading to record your thoughts. For each row (R, !, and ?) you will need at least two passages written in the left-hand side. For each of these passages, you need to write a well-developed paragraph in the right-hand side. A well-developed paragraph makes connections by interpreting facts and their significance—not just stating facts.

Although dialectical journals focus on reading, it is important for you to put significant energy and time into making connections and communicating clearly and effectively in your observations and writing. Do not simply state facts from the text—*interpret these facts and state their significance.*

ORAL HISTORY RESOURCES

ORAL HISTORY ORGANIZATIONS/ARCHIVES

ORAL HISTORY ASSOCIATION: The Oral History Association, established in 1966, seeks to bring together all persons interested in oral history as a way of collecting and interpreting human memories to foster knowledge and human dignity. (*www.oralhistory.org*)

STORYCORPS: StoryCorps is an independent nonprofit whose mission is to provide Americans of all backgrounds and beliefs with the opportunity to record, share, and preserve the stories of our lives. (*www.storycorps.org*)

LIBRARY OF CONGRESS: WPA American Life Histories from the Federal Writes Project, and Recordings (*lcweb2.loc.gov/wpaintro/wpahome.html*). Oral History for Educators (lesson plans, etc.) (*learning.loc.gov/learn/lessons/oralhist/ohhome.html*)

COLUMBIA CENTER FOR ORAL HISTORY: The Columbia University Center for Oral History is one of the world's leading centers for the practice and teaching of oral history. Its archive, located in the Columbia University Libraries and open to the public, holds more than 8,000 interviews, in audio, video, and text formats, on a wide variety of subjects. (*library.columbia.edu/indiv/ccoh.html*)

CENTER FOR DIGITAL STORYTELLING: The Center for Digital Storytelling is a California-based nonprofit arts organization rooted in the art of personal storytelling. They assist people of all ages in using the tools of digital media to craft, record, share, and value the stories of individuals and communities. (*www.storycenter.org*)

CHICAGO HISTORY MUSEUM: THE STUDS TERKEL / WFMT ORAL HISTORY ARCHIVES: Audio recordings of interviews, readings, and musical programs aired during Studs Terkel's tenure at WFMT Radio from the early 1950s through 1999 are part of the museum's collection. Over five decades, Terkel interviewed individuals from every walk of life. These interviews narrate the cultural, literary, and political history of Chicago and the United States. (*www.chicagohs.org/research/aboutcollection/archivesmanuscripts*)

BOOKS

Terkel, Studs. *Working: People Talk About What They Do All Day and How They Feel About What They Do*. The New Press, 2003 (reissue).

Ayers, Rick. *Working: A Teaching Guide*. The New Press, 2001.

Terkel, Studs. *Hard Times: An Oral History of the Great Depression*. The New Press, 2005 (reissue).

Zinn, Howard, and Anthony Arnove. *Voices of a People's History of the United States*. Seven Stories Press, 2004.

Griffin, Joanne. *Redefining Black Power: Reflections on the State of Black America*. City Lights Publishers, 2012.

Isay, David. *Listening Is an Act of Love: A Celebration of American Life from the StoryCorps Project*. Penguin Books, 2007.

Jones, LeAlan, Lloyd Newman, with David Isay. *Our America: Life and Death on the South Side of Chicago*. Washington Square Press/Pocket Books, 1997.

Taylor, Craig. *Londoners: The Days and Nights of London Now —As Told by Those Who Love It, Hate It, Live It, Left It, and Long for It*. Ecco/Harper Collins, 2012.

Ritchie, Donald. *Doing Oral History*. Oxford University Press, 2003 (second edition).

ORAL HISTORY–BASED PLAYS

Kaufman, Moises et al. *The Laramie Project*. Vintage Books, 2001.

Smith, Deavere Anna. *Twilight: Los Angeles, 1992*. Anchor Books, 1994.

Blank, Jessica, Erik Jensen. *The Exonerated*. Faber and Faber, 2003.

Blank, Jessica, Erik Jensen. *Aftermath*. Dramatists Play Service, 2010 (acting edition).

FACING HISTORY AND OURSELVES: Facing History and Ourselves is an international educational and professional development organization whose mission is to engage students of diverse backgrounds in an examination of racism, prejudice, and anti-Semitism in order to promote the development of a more humane and informed citizenry. (*www.facinghistory.org*)

TEACHING TOLERANCE: A place to find thought-provoking news, conversation, and support for those who care about diversity, equal opportunity, and respect for difference in schools. (*www.tolerance.org*)

THE FRED T. KOREMATSU INSTITUTE FOR CIVIL RIGHTS AND EDUCATION: The mission of the Fred T. Korematsu Institute for Civil Rights and Education is to advance pan-ethnic civil rights and human rights through education. (*www.korematsuinstitute.org*)

THE CHOICES PROGRAM: The Choices for the 21st Century Education Program is a national education initiative developed at Brown University's Watson Institute for International Studies. The Choices Program provides teaching resources on historical and current international issues, offers professional development for classroom teachers, and sponsors programs that engage students beyond the classroom. (*www.choices.edu*)

STRATEGIC LITERACY INITIATIVE: The Strategic Literacy Initiative is a professional development and research project of WestEd. The project serves middle- and high-school teachers and administrators, literacy coaches, and teacher educators nationally. (*www.wested.org/cs/we/view/pj/179*)

ZINN EDUCATION PROJECT: The Zinn Education Project promotes and supports the use of Howard Zinn's best-selling book *A People's History of the United States* and other materials for teaching a people's history in middle- and high-school classrooms across the country. The website offers more than one hundred free, downloadable lessons and articles organized by theme, time period, and reading level. (*www.zinnedproject.org*)

TEACHING FOR CHANGE: Teaching for Change provides teachers and parents with the tools to transform schools into centers of justice where students learn to read, write, and change the world. (*www.teachingforchange.org*)

RETHINKING SCHOOLS: Rethinking Schools is a nonprofit, independent publisher of educational materials, advocating the reform of elementary and secondary education, with a strong emphasis on issues of equity and social justice. (*www.rethinkingschools.org*)

NATIONAL COUNCIL FOR THE SOCIAL STUDIES (NCSS): Social studies educators teach students the content knowledge, intellectual skills, and civic values necessary for fulfilling the duties of citizenship in a participatory democracy. The mission of National Council for the Social Studies is to provide leadership, service, and support for all social studies educators. (*www.socialstudies.org*)

NATIONAL COUNCIL OF TEACHERS OF ENGLISH (NCTE): The Council promotes the development of literacy, the use of language to construct personal and public worlds and to achieve full participation in society, through the learning and teaching of English and the related arts and sciences of language. (*www.ncte.org*)

NATIONAL ASSOCIATION FOR MULTICULTURAL EDUCATION: NAME is a non-profit organization that advances and advocates for equity and social justice through multicultural education. (*nameorg.org*)

SURVIVING JUSTICE
America's Wrongfully Convicted and Exonerated
Edited by Lola Vollen and Dave Eggers
Foreword by Scott Turow

These oral histories prove that the problem of wrongful conviction is far-reaching and very real. Through a series of all-too-common circumstances—eyewitness misidentification, inept defense lawyers, coercive interrogation—the lives of these men and women of all different backgrounds were irreversibly disrupted. In *Surviving Justice*, thirteen exonerees describe their experiences—the events that led to their convictions, their years in prison, and the process of adjusting to their new lives outside.

VOICES FROM THE STORM
The People of New Orleans on Hurricane Katrina and Its Aftermath
Edited by Chris Ying and Lola Vollen

Voices from the Storm is a chronological account of the worst natural disaster in modern American history. Thirteen New Orleanians describe the days leading up to Hurricane Katrina, the storm itself, and the harrowing confusion of the days and months afterward. Their stories weave and intersect, ultimately creating an eye-opening portrait of courage in the face of terror, and of hope amid nearly complete devastation.

UNDERGROUND AMERICA
Narratives of Undocumented Lives
Edited by Peter Orner
Foreword by Luis Alberto Urrea

They arrive from around the world for countless reasons. Many come simply to make a living. Others are fleeing persecution in their native countries. But by living and working in the United States without legal status, millions of immigrants risk deportation and imprisonment. They live underground, with little protection from exploitation at the hands of human smugglers, employers, or law enforcement. *Underground America* presents the remarkable oral histories of men and women struggling to carve a life for themselves in the United States. In 2010, *Underground America* was translated into Spanish and released as *En las Sombras de Estados Unidos*.

OUT OF EXILE
The Abducted and Displaced People of Sudan
Edited by Craig Walzer
Additional interviews and an introduction by Dave Eggers and Valentino Achak Deng

Millions of people have fled from conflicts and persecution in all parts of Sudan, and many thousands more have been enslaved as human spoils of war. In *Out of Exile*, refugees and abductees recount their escapes from the wars in Darfur and South Sudan, from political and religious persecution, and from abduction by militias. They tell of life before the war, and of the hope that they might someday find peace again.

HOPE DEFERRED

Narratives of Zimbabwean Lives

Edited by Peter Orner and Annie Holmes

Foreword by Brian Chikwava

The sixth volume in the Voice of Witness series presents the narratives of Zimbabweans whose lives have been affected by the country's political, economic, and human rights crises. This book asks the question: How did a country with so much promise—a stellar education system, a growing middle class of professionals, a sophisticated economic infrastructure, a liberal constitution, and an independent judiciary—go so wrong?

NOWHERE TO BE HOME

Narratives from Survivors of Burma's Military Regime

Edited by Maggie Lemere and Zoë West

Foreword by Mary Robinson

Decades of military oppression in Burma have led to the systematic destruction of thousands of ethnic minority villages, a standing army with one of the world's highest number of child soldiers, and the displacement of millions of people. *Nowhere to Be Home* is an eye-opening collection of oral histories exposing the realities of life under military rule. In their own words, men and women from Burma describe their lives in the country that Human Rights Watch has called "the textbook example of a police state."

PATRIOT ACTS

Narratives of Post-9/11 Injustice

Edited by Alia Malek

Foreword by Karen Korematsu

Patriot Acts tells the stories of men and women who have been needlessly swept up in the War on Terror. In their own words, narrators recount personal experiences of the post-9/11 backlash that have deeply altered their lives and communities. *Patriot Acts* illuminates these experiences in a compelling collection of eighteen oral histories from men and women who have found themselves subject to a wide range of human and civil rights abuses—from rendition and torture, to workplace discrimination, bullying, FBI surveillance, and harassment.

INSIDE THIS PLACE, NOT OF IT

Narratives from Women's Prisons

Edited by Ayelet Waldman and Robin Levi

Foreword by Michelle Alexander

Inside This Place, Not of It reveals some of the most egregious human rights violations within women's prisons in the United States. In their own words, the thirteen narrators in this book recount their lives leading up to incarceration and their experiences inside—ranging from forced sterilization and shackling during childbirth, to physical and sexual abuse by prison staff. Together, their testimonies illustrate the harrowing struggles for survival that women in prison must endure.

THROWING STONES AT THE MOON
Narratives from Colombians Displaced by Violence
Edited by Sibylla Brodzinsky and Max Schoening
Foreword by Íngrid Betancourt

For nearly five decades, Colombia has been embroiled in internal armed conflict among guerrilla groups, paramilitary militias, and the country's own military. Civilians in Colombia face a range of abuses from all sides, including killings, disappearances, and rape—and more than four million have been forced to flee their homes. The oral histories in *Throwing Stones at the Moon* describe the most widespread of Colombia's human rights crises: forced displacement. Speakers recount life before displacement, the reasons for their flight, and their struggle to rebuild their lives.

REFUGEE HOTEL
Compiled and edited by Juliet Linderman and Gabriele Stabile

Refugee Hotel is a groundbreaking collection of photography and interviews that documents the arrival of refugees in the United States. Evocative images are coupled with moving testimonies from people describing their first days in the U.S., the lives they've left behind, and the new communities they've since created.

FROM OUR DONOR

Dear Readers,

First of all, thank you. As educators and community leaders, you have a calling to bring greater meaning and humanity into your classrooms and homes, bringing immeasurable value to the community.

We see how challenging it is for young people to be fully engaged in their classes, their school communities, and in the world around them. This is a disconnection of the heart. And we feel that a critical purpose of education is to develop the heart, and its ability to deeply see, understand, and feel kinship with others. From this comes the urge to become authentic, confident, and to offer our gifts to the world.

Storytelling has always been a powerful way to learn about ourselves, develop empathy with others, discover our reasons for being, and to build community. We are proud to provide seed funding for the Voice of Witness Education Program, as it shares this way of knowing with you and so many others. We believe that the Voice of Witness team's passion, and their deep understanding of the power of stories, will foster awakening and constructive change in the world.

Caroline Pfohl
Founder
Hemera Foundation

Founded in 2007, Hemera is a philanthropic organization dedicated to introducing secular contemplative views and practices into mainstream society, focusing on education, children, and the arts. Hemera generously supported the first edition of The Power of the Story.